# Climate-Ready Business

# Climate-Ready Business

## *Responsible Growth and Profitability*

Valentina Fomenko

**┃╻┃BEP**
BUSINESS EXPERT PRESS
*Leader in applied, concise business books*

First published in 2025 by
Business Expert Press, LLC
222 East 46th Street, New York, NY 10017
www.businessexpertpress.com

ISBN-13: 978-1-63742-790-3 (paperback)
ISBN-13: 978-1-63742-791-0 (e-book)

Business Expert Press Environmental and Social Sustainability for Business Advantage

First edition: 2025

10 9 8 7 6 5 4 3 2 1

**EU SAFETY REPRESENTATIVE**
Mare Nostrum Group B.V.
Mauritskade 21D
1091 GC Amsterdam
The Netherlands
gpsr@mare-nostrum.co.uk

# Description

The pressure on the private sector to act on climate change is immense—yet, despite good intentions, many companies are stalled by fragmented efforts, unclear priorities, and mounting risk. Without a clear strategy, climate efforts remain scattered, reactive, and easy to derail.

*Climate-Ready Business* delivers the missing playbook. It equips you with a practical, end-to-end framework for building a climate-ready organization. Written for business leaders aiming to turn climate commitment into competitive advantage, it provides an actionable, step-by-step guide to building a cohesive, future-proof strategy—without burying you in technical detail.

By following this field-tested roadmap, your company can transition from scrambling to comply to leading: products and services designed for a low-carbon world, stakeholders who trust your stewardship, risks contained, talent energized, and your organization prepared to meet future challenges.

# Contents

Acknowledgments..................................................................ix

Introduction ......................................................................xi

Chapter 1  The Rising Tide............................................1

Chapter 2  Reduce Your Footprint .......................................17

Chapter 3  Think Life Cycle ...........................................39

Chapter 4  Understand and Manage Climate Risks...........................55

Chapter 5  Discover Climate Opportunities...............................73

Chapter 6  Keep Yourself Accountable .................................93

Chapter 7  Partner With Stakeholders....................................109

Chapter 8  Survive This Sea Change and the Next ..........................129

Notes.............................................................................145

References ........................................................................155

About the Author.................................................................169

Index .............................................................................171

# Acknowledgments

This book stands as a testament to the power of shared purpose. My deepest gratitude goes to business leaders, entrepreneurs, and changemakers at the forefront of sustainable transformation, including my clients and fellow professionals who generously shared their insights—your experiences fueled this project and guided its direction.

To my husband, John Bautista: your love and encouragement kept my spirit strong through all the ups and downs of writing this book. My parents, Marina and Georgy Fomenko, set the bar high and taught me to follow my calling through global currents and personal shifts; your passion and wise counsel carried this project forward and across the finish line.

A special thanks to the teams at Strategy DNA, Inc. and The Institute for Sustainable Innovation for their unmatched resilience and dedication to climate strategy work. I am equally grateful to those who provided detailed, constructive feedback on various chapters—Les Joslin, Robin Colucci, Otis Fuqua, and Dylan Hoffman. I could not have done this without your sharp feedback and steady support.

Finally, my heartfelt appreciation goes to the team at Business Expert Press—especially Scott Isenberg and Robert Sroufe—for shepherding this book to the readers who need it and for your thoughtful guidance.

# Introduction

Today, the private sector faces two major mandates, one ancient and the other relatively new. The first, to make money. The second, to take action against climate change. After decades of inaction, companies are increasingly responding to the latter charge. Between 2019 and 2020, the number of companies committing to net-zero carbon footprint goals doubled,[1] with 400 of the world's 2,000 largest public companies making this commitment.[2] Smaller companies have followed suit, with over 1,200 small and midsize enterprises in 65 countries making net-zero commitments since late 2020 alone.[3]

Yet, for decades, business leaders have viewed these as mutually exclusive goals, and many still do. This might explain why, of the thousands of companies committing to achieve net-zero or science-based carbon emission reduction targets, after years of investor pressure, only 59 percent actually identify the key decarbonization actions they will take to accomplish their goals, and just over 20 percent quantify their impacts.[4] Even when companies release plans, they don't always follow through, or the plans they release are vague and reach too far into the future for them to be implemented in a way that will make a difference in the near term. And even then, the small percentage of companies that have a reasonable, actionable plan often either fail or don't go as far as they should.

This dismissive stance toward the climate constitutes a massive mistake. Climate change poses unprecedented amounts of risk to companies. In 2019, the 215 largest companies in the world reported almost $1 trillion at risk due to the impacts of climate change.[5] If we extrapolate this number to account for all private and public companies, the total value at risk due to climate change could climb up to $15 trillion. At the same time, climate change presents a tremendous business opportunity. In June of 2021, the International Energy Agency estimated the total investment opportunity of global decarbonization at $100 trillion[6] and that does not include the opportunities companies create for themselves by adapting to such new conditions, as taking advantage of new shipping routes, infrastructure hardening projects, or introducing new insurance products. It's clear that to ensure the profitability of their businesses, not to mention the survival of the planet, business leaders need to prioritize their climate strategies instead of shying away from the problem. And it's equally clear that most businesses have no idea how to do that.

The harsh reality is that leaders at many companies, large and small, seem lost in a fog when it comes to climate issues. The prevalent societal narrative urges them to take responsibility for environmental and societal impacts stretching far beyond their usual scope of concern. Indeed, we are in our full right to expect more. Yet many—especially in the United States—are only now waking up to the need to address climate-related issues in a systematic way. They acknowledge the coming storm but struggle to decipher exactly what to do about it. Missing is a straightforward roadmap to help them traverse the unfamiliar territory of climate action. Amid the buzzwords and lofty goals surrounding corporate sustainability, there is a genuine need for guidance.

To every passionate sustainability officer, dedicated environmental advocate, and individual feeling caught up in the "us versus them" dynamic of the climate change conversation: This book is for you. Whether you're part of a large conglomerate, a medium-sized enterprise, or a small budding firm, the messages here seek to speak directly to your experience—and your challenges. I recognize that the conversation around climate change often feels polarized, and it's easy to feel lost or chastised amidst the noise. This is your invitation to dig deeper, to understand the underlying psychology and value systems that drive these discussions. Let's move beyond the limited circle of elite sustainability leadership and truly democratize the conversation. Together, we can bridge divides, nurture understanding, and pave a way forward that's inclusive and transformative. Your voice matters, and through these pages, I hope to amplify it.

Over the years, I have drawn from my training as an environmental scientist and business strategist in working with multiple government bodies, international NGOs, and Fortune 500 companies to help them navigate these choppy waters. I have seen many companies, both large and small, struggling to get their climate programs off the ground. Corporate leaders tend to see the myriad topics related to climate change as obscure and excessively technical and thus relegate them to a growing army of consultants.

These observations fueled my decision to write this book, which focuses on the business side of climate change solutions, outlining what leaders and organizations can do to address climate change while ensuring the short-term profitability and long-term sustainability of their companies. To succeed, companies need to integrate climate considerations into the very DNA of their organizations. As with all transformative endeavors, it is essential that these initiatives are approached with care and strategic insight. For that to happen, companies must rethink the very way they approach their strategy, operations, product or service development, financial planning, risk management, and virtually every other business function. Tactical solutions without a new strategic foundation are neither truly effective nor sustainable in the long term. I will provide the definitive blueprint for this urgent transformation.

Central to this blueprint is the idea of corporate climate readiness. Similar to the way the military uses this word, readiness is the function of organizations' ability to adapt to environmental changes, market conditions, and new regulations; get comfortable dealing with complex data; and look for opportunities amidst challenges. Simply put, it's about being ready and adaptable for what's coming in our changing climate. To maximize profits and minimize environmental impact, climate readiness requires organizations to treat environmental concerns and climate change as one of the core pillars of their business strategy instead of as an afterthought.

Focusing on climate readiness takes us a step beyond the more prevalent concepts of climate mitigation, adaptation, or resilience. More than just taking action to limit the menace of mercury rising, find ways to thrive in changing conditions, or bounce back from disruptions, readiness embodies a proactive approach to not only face but also leverage the impending challenges of climate change. Akin to a map of the forest at the trailhead, this book will help you grasp the bigger picture of how climate change intersects with business, assist in charting your path with discernment and confidence, and illuminate the silver linings and opportunities that arise amidst challenges. In essence, it's about turning threats into advantages.

This book is meant to be a friendly guide rather than a stern lecture. Think of it as a companion in a journey through the maze of scientific terminology, reporting requirements, strategic frameworks, and implementation approaches. Although it incorporates numerous examples from my own consulting practice and from across the business world, it's not a mere collection of cases but rather a straightforward guide designed to empower those making climate-conscious decisions.

The book consists of eight chapters. Chapter 1 provides an overview of the challenges companies face in dealing with the impacts of climate change. Chapters 2 through 7 offer analysis and actionable strategies for companies to adapt to climate change in the following key areas:

- How to identify and prioritize solutions and investments required for reducing their carbon footprint.
- Why it is important to assess—and address—climate considerations through the entire value chain, and how to do it.
- How to identify and quantify the risks that climate change poses to their companies, and what steps they can take to manage that risk and save millions of dollars.
- How to take advantage of new business opportunities presented by the fight against climate change—and the urgent need to adapt to the changes that are already underway.
- How to collaborate with stakeholders, including community members, customers, and suppliers, to develop new approaches that maximize profits while minimizing climate impacts—and increase their ability to adapt to climate change.
- How to anticipate and stay ahead of new climate-related regulations, saving money and situating a company at the forefront of the fight against climate change—and helping communities thrive in the new climate reality.
- How to implement new company-wide climate initiatives.

To make this information even more actionable, I invite you to visit the Business Expert Press website, where you'll find additional practical tools, such as the Corporate Climate Readiness Assessment developed by the team at Strategy DNA, Inc. This way, you will start with a clear understanding of your organization's gaps in strategic thinking and planning, governance, culture and values, and operational processes as they relate to climate readiness. Knowing where to focus your efforts enables early wins while establishing a solid roadmap for the future.

As time passes, this book will feel more and more like a historical read. Yet, I hope its core lessons will remain relevant and timeless. The pragmatic approach I advocate can serve as a template for addressing myriad challenges, some current and some not yet foreseen. The climate issue encapsulates the complex web of problems that are bound to challenge us in the future—from technological complexities to deep ideological divides and unprecedented levels of uncertainty. My objective is to furnish a practical framework to tackle the quandaries of today—and tomorrow. This is why Chapter 8 zooms out to future crises and explains how you can leverage the lessons learned from fighting and adapting to climate change to anticipate and respond to the next crisis faster—and better than your competitors.

The discourse around climate is noisy. The heightened chatter around the topic is often like that of an overenthusiastic uncle at family reunions, warning everyone about the impending doom of, well, everything. Yet, amidst these emotions, there lies a beacon of hope—a yearning not just for a rejuvenated earth but also for the transformation of our collective spirit. Our shared concern about climate is proof that we all hope for a better world, a brighter tomorrow. So, let's roll up our sleeves, trade stories from the trenches, maybe share a chuckle or two about our missteps, and get to work. There's hope, and it starts with us.

# CHAPTER 1

# The Rising Tide

How did I get roped into the intricacies of corporate climate strategy? A few years ago, one of the largest fertilizer producers in the world faced a reputational challenge. For a long time, CDP, formerly known as Climate Disclosure Project, the world's leading climate reporting platform, had given it an "F"—meaning it hadn't provided CDP with any data. The company wore the grade like a scarlet letter. And investors and customers started to notice. Their C-suite was receiving calls from frustrated investors who demanded more transparency of the company's carbon footprint, its efforts to mitigate its environmental impact, and its plan for adapting to climate change. The F from the CDP told the public and their customers, accurately or not, that they were failing in all of these areas. They needed to change this perception. At first, they tried to handle the situation on their own, but as they waded through the CDP's voluminous, cryptic instructions, they became overwhelmed.

Feeling this pressure, they brought in consultants. Within our first few meetings, it was clear that the string of Fs and all the reputational fallout that accompanied them were merely symptoms of a larger issue. This fertilizer company, like most other companies, had failed to comprehend the full impact of climate change on its business. They did have a strong history of complying with various environmental regulations and employee health and safety standards, but climate just wasn't on their radar. What little climate action they did take was handled by their Environmental Health and Safety group, which effectively meant it was cordoned off from the rest of the organization.

In other words, they had failed to develop what I call a climate-readiness strategy. Over the course of our work together, our team helped them move from their reactive, disjointed climate response to a proactive climate strategy. They developed a robust climate-readiness apparatus that would allow them to predict and manage the impacts of both environmental changes and regulatory shifts, rapidly adapt to new market conditions, and take advantage of new opportunities that climate change might bring about while reducing their environmental impact. Several years into its "climate journey," the company enjoys a well-deserved reputation as a climate leader in its industry. Climate issues get attention directly from the Chair of the Board of Directors, with the Chief Financial Officer overseeing all climate-readiness work. While this transformation took commitment and effort, it was hardly rocket science. It can serve as a blueprint and a source of inspiration for many others.

The rest of this book will examine how to develop and implement a climate-readiness strategy. But before we get to that, we should look at the costs associated with continuing to ignore climate change. It can be tempting to downplay the impact of climate change and cleave climate considerations from your business decisions. However, that is simply no longer possible. In recent decades, climate change has impacted natural and human systems on all continents, in all oceans. Between 1880 and 2012, the average global temperature increased by 0.85°C. The oceans warmed; ice, snow, and glaciers melted; and sea levels rose by 19 cm. Since 1979, the amount of ice cover in the Arctic Ocean has decreased each decade by about 500,000 square kilometers. Given current greenhouse gas (GHG) concentrations and emissions, it is likely that, by the end of this century, global average temperatures will have risen 1°C to 2°C above 1990 levels and 1.5°C to 2.5°C above preindustrial levels. Scientists estimate that, by 2065, global mean sea level will rise by 24 to 30 cm, and 40 to 63 cm by 2100, compared to 1986 to 2005 levels. Most effects of climate change will persist for several centuries, even if GHG emissions cease completely.

But this book is not just about busier hurricane seasons or longer droughts. Plenty of important books are available on those subjects. This book is about the critical relationship between climate change and the global economy and, ultimately, your bottom line.

## Your Bottom Line

If you lead or own a business, you've probably already felt the impact of climate change. Yet, because of the years of corporate obfuscation about the severity of the climate crisis, many companies fail to see the current impact of climate change or even take climate change seriously. Some business leaders believe that new regulations will simply wash away with the next shift in the political tide. Or that they can continue "business as usual" while they deploy legal teams to find new ways to circumvent legal limits. Or, perhaps more well-meaning leaders worry that developing a climate strategy in earnest will lead to spending large amounts of resources on what might ultimately turn out to be a futile effort. But any of these responses would prove to be a massively costly mistake, and there is an overwhelming amount of data that proves it.

According to an assessment by the Intergovernmental Panel on Climate Change (IPCC), climate change directly impacts 70 percent of all economic sectors worldwide.[1] In the United States, experts expect every 1°C increase in average global temperature to cause a 1.2 percent decline in the annual gross domestic product (GDP).[2] *National Mortgage News* estimates that climate change will put $450 billion worth of residential properties in the United States at risk by 2050.[3] The United States is not exceptional in this regard. The Swiss Re Institute, an insurance underwriter, conducted a stress test of 48 economies around the world and found that in a scenario with a 3.2°C temperature increase over preindustrial levels, China would lose 24 percent of its GDP by midcentury; the United States, Canada, and the United Kingdom would all lose around 10 percent GDP; and Europe overall would lose around 11 percent. The same test found that even if we meet the goals of less than a 2°C increase, as set in the Paris Climate Accord, we will still lose 4 percent of global GDP.[4]

Most of that GDP loss will result from direct physical changes to the environment such as higher temperatures and severe weather events. Higher temperatures already increase our energy and water use, which have made blackouts and brownouts more common and threaten our long-term reliable energy supply.[5] Extreme heat impacts vulnerable workers, reduces labor availability across the board (particularly in the cases of emergency operations, construction, and health care workers), supports the spread of diseases like Lyme disease, dengue, chikungunya, and Zika, and can damage sensitive manufacturing components.[6,7] According to an analysis reported in the *Journal of Environmental Economics,* in 2017, a single day at a plant in China with temperatures higher than 90°C cost the plant more than $10,000 as it hampered the performance of workers and equipment.[8]

Severe weather events can wreak havoc on modern supply chains, characterized by their global reach and reduced inventories for just-in-time production. In 2011, severe flooding in Thailand disrupted the supply chain of 14,500 companies, causing total insured losses estimated between $15 billion and $20 billion.[9] In 2010, a drought in Russia produced wildfires that destroyed an estimated $15 billion worth of crops. The resulting export restrictions increased global crop prices.[10] As much as severe weather impacts international industry and trade, climate change often hits small- and medium-sized businesses the hardest. An average of 25 percent of such businesses do not reopen after disasters such as hurricanes, droughts, or extreme heat waves.[11]

Overall, data from CDP shows that the world's largest companies face one trillion dollars in climate-related risks.[12] Even if extreme weather doesn't directly strike a company, the risk is enough to hurt its bottom line. Research shows that companies with higher climate-related risks face a higher cost of capital, making it harder for them to borrow money and lowering their share prices.[13]

It's not just the climate itself that can hurt your bottom line, but also a failure to take climate action. According to GreenBiz, companies that don't voluntarily report their carbon emissions lose up to $1.5 million every year in interest repayments.[14] That, plus research shows that companies that voluntarily report their climate data and carefully track the actions they take to mitigate their impact have greater and cheaper access to capital.[15] Failure to capitalize on these incentives (and avoid penalties) adds up to a constant, substantial drain on profits, often without anyone realizing it.

Then, of course, we must consider the customers. According to a 2020 study by IBM and the National Retail Federation, almost 70 percent of North American consumers think it is important that a brand is sustainable or eco-friendly.[16] Customer boycotts and employee activism have spiked. In July 2020, 38 percent of Americans were boycotting a company for its policy positions, treatment of employees, political donations, or other reasons.[17] In coming years, as the public continues to grow more concerned about climate change, both numbers will likely only go up, meaning continued unsustainable practices will prevent you from accessing a sizable chunk of the market.

Companies with a weak climate record also face legal repercussions. In response to more severe weather events, communities have filed lawsuits against fossil fuel corporations to hold them financially accountable for damage caused by climate change. These "climate liability" cases rely on research from the Carbon Majors report, which links carbon and GHG emissions to individual emitters. The report traces 71 percent of global warming gases to just 100 companies, the "Carbon Majors."[18] Improvements in real-time data collection have provided plaintiffs in climate liability cases with new evidence to link climate-related disasters to individual sources of emissions.

Investors, regulators, and other authorities have ratcheted up the pressure on businesses to act. As of this writing, mandatory climate disclosures seem inevitable. In 2021, G7 finance ministers met in London to declare their support for "mandatory climate-related financial disclosures" for public companies across the largest advanced economies.[19] This move followed eight years of mandatory GHG emissions disclosures by companies listed on the main market of the London Stock Exchange (LSE). In 2020, the LSE main market mandated additional reporting about climate-related risks for each listed company. In the United States, the Greenhouse Gas Reporting Program (GHGRP), administered by the U.S. Environmental Protection Agency (EPA), already mandates GHG reporting by emitters of over 25,000 metric tons of $CO_2e^*$ per year, as well as fuel and industrial gas suppliers, and $CO_2$ injection sites.[20] Australia has had mandatory

---

* It is comon practice to use carbon dioxide "equivalent" as a common metric for all greenhouse gases in order to account for the variation in their global warming potential.

emissions reporting for its largest GHG emitters under its National Greenhouse and Energy Reporting Scheme (NGERS) since 2007.[21]

The European Green Deal, approved in 2020, has had a drastic impact on companies across Europe and those looking to access the European market. As of this writing, the European Union seems poised to implement a Carbon Border Adjustment Mechanism (CBAM), applicable to imported products and services, which would essentially apply a carbon tax on imports that equals the current carbon tax in Europe. For some companies, tax liabilities like this could become a matter of life and death. According to some estimates, this tax could reduce foreign producers' overall profits by about 20 percent. For producers of carbon-intensive products like flat-rolled steel, the loss would be even greater, around 40 percent.[22]

Then, there is the cost associated with having to report on the climate impacts, which can be substantial. Right now, only the world's largest companies by market capitalization have to report their activities to the CDP. These companies must now report not only on their carbon footprint but on myriad other topics including climate risks, opportunities, governance, and stakeholder engagement. Refusing to report this information results in an "F" grade from CDP. Even if your company is smaller, CDP may still request your information if you work with one of its 200 "supply chain members," which are some of the largest purchasing organizations in the world. Over 15,000 companies have received these requests. Many have been caught flat-footed. Every other publicly traded company will likely soon need to report as well. In March 2024, the Securities and Exchange Commission (SEC) in the United States adopted its long-awaited rules requiring public corporations to include climate liabilities, risks, and opportunities in their disclosures to investors. In Europe, the EU Corporate Sustainability Reporting Directive (CSRD) mandates companies with operations in the EU to report on their environmental and social impact and activities starting in 2024. This includes information on climate-related metrics and targets, strategy, and risk management. In a similar move, the Climate Corporate Data Accountability Act (SB 253) and the Climate-Related Financial Risk Act (SB 261) adopted in California in 2023 require large companies doing business in the state to annually report their GHG emissions starting in 2026.

In the coming years, the climate will have an ever-greater impact on business operations. Despite ever-changing political tides, climate regulations and societal pressures are here to stay. Eventually, all companies will have to navigate the climate maze, and the sooner all businesses get on board, the better. Does this mean you should drop everything and place climate in the crosshairs of your strategic focus? For a few companies, the answer may be yes. Most, however, will face less drastic disruptions and will require more measured responses. The most important thing is that you act and make sure that any action you take remains aligned with your overall strategy. Everything you do on climate will help you survive—and thrive—in a world constantly grappling with new disruptions.

## Navigating the Wild West of Climate Strategy

Once you've decided to act, you must figure out how to act. The 2010s and early 2020s were what I call the "Wild West" phase of corporate climate change strategy. It was a new frontier, still mostly unexplored, with few laws to guide behavior. Several companies and organizations have scrambled to fill the vacuum of understanding. Consulting firms dedicated to helping companies navigate the new climate reality have popped up. Likewise, hundreds of organizations have introduced sustainability standards and reporting frameworks that include climate-related metrics. The boom in these frameworks has resulted in a veritable alphabet soup of acronyms: SBTi, CDP, SASB, CDSB, MSCI, TCFD, GRESB,[†] and so on. Seemingly every few

---

[†] The Science Based Targets initiative (SBTi) is a collaboration of several global nonprofits to set science-based climate targets. CDP, formerly Climate Disclosure Project, is an international nonprofit focused on helping companies and cities disclose their climate and environmental impact. The Sustainability Accounting Standards Board (SASB) is a nonprofit founded to develop sustainability accounting standards. Climate Disclosure Standards Board (CDSB), until January 2022, was a consortium of businesses and nonprofits working to align climate reporting frameworks. MSCI Inc. is a U.S. finance company providing comprehensive sustainability ratings, which include

months, a new rating is born, while the existing frameworks regularly shift.

This results in widespread confusion and anxiety. Smaller companies often lack the resources to understand the dozens of frameworks, much less use them to report their climate impacts. While larger companies have more resources, they also have far more activity to report and metrics to track. And even with the resources, they often don't know where to start. So, they rely on metrics and heuristics that may not be relevant or even accurate, and this reliance draws the ire of regulators and watchdog groups alike.[23, 24]

## Climate Ratings

Increasingly, investors look to climate ratings to decide if a company is a safe investment. Climate ratings are based on the reporting standards, and like the reporting standards, there are too many ratings with too much variance between them to know which to choose. Each rating agency has its own methods and scales, meaning a company might have an excellent rating with one agency and a lackluster rating with another, regardless of how well they are responding to climate change. It should come as no surprise that, in a survey of 50 asset managers, 20 reported using data from at least 4 climate ratings agencies, and 30 admitted to developing their own ratings.[25]

Because these reporting standards are so confusing, companies often ignore them completely. Or, they take the opposite approach and orient every part of their climate strategy around the frameworks. If —and when—the SEC rolls out its own reporting framework, many companies will be tempted to adopt the reporting-centric approach. Widely recognized as potentially the most significant change in public company reporting since Sarbanes-Oxley,[‡] the implementation of the SEC's framework will prompt companies to hire armies of consultants

---

climate-related components. Task Force on Climate-Related Financial Disclosures (TCFD) is a group representing both preparers and users of financial disclosures, created to develop guidelines for disclosing information on climate risks and opportunities. Global ESG Benchmark for Real Assets (GRESB) is an investor-led nonprofit focused on providing climate and sustainability data on real estate and infrastructure.

(likely from big accounting firms) to address pressing issues around compliance while leaving deeper strategic conversations on the back burner. But such a strategy completely misses the point. Satisfying reporting requirements and getting a decent rating can keep you in the good graces of ESG-focused investors and regulators. But do not overestimate the importance of reporting. Stopping there would mean missed opportunities.

For many companies, collecting relevant data and thinking through their exposure to climate-related risks may kickstart the conversation around an appropriate response in the mid and short-term. But this approval only goes so far. The real goal is to mitigate your company's climatic impact while adapting to ongoing climatic changes, not to chase ever-shifting reporting demands.

Ultimately, these reporting mechanisms should be viewed as merely tools—stepping stones toward developing a comprehensive climate strategy for your company. They can help you assess your climate impact and introduce a climate dimension into your strategy, operations, and decision making. They can also help you communicate and validate your climate strategy to other organizations and individuals.

The way out of the metric morass is to identify which tools assist your company the most. Some have a clear global relevance; some point to local impacts. Some focus on meeting the needs of specific audiences and agendas. Yet, for all the diversity, there are two essential things your company needs to track and report on: your contribution to climate change and the climate-related risks you face.

## CDP and TCFD

The current dominant reporting framework to measure carbon footprint and environmental impact currently is the CDP, formerly known as the Climate Disclosure Project. CDP gathers information on GHG emissions, water usage, and impact on forests and other ecosystems from the world's largest companies and their suppliers. They then distribute

‡ The Sarbanes–Oxley Act of 2002 is a federal law in the United States that mandated stringent practices in corporate financial reporting and recordkeeping.

that information to investors and consumers. CDP also runs a similar carbon footprint reporting program for cities. Over 750 cities and 7,000 companies with over 50 percent of global market capitalization disclosed environmental data through CDP in 2018. Even if you choose not to disclose through CDP, or if you are too small to end up on their radar, they are a great source of best practices in measuring, reporting, and minimizing climate impact for any company, regardless of size.

In the climate risks realm, the Taskforce for Climate-related Financial Disclosures (TCFD) emerged as the dominant player through the backing of several high-profile investors. Michael Bloomberg chairs its 31-member board, which includes bankers, representatives of chemical and manufacturing organizations, accounting standards bodies, S&P, Moody's, and the Sustainability Accounting Standards Board (SASB). TCFD asks the right questions of companies, often for the first time—it probes the depth of a company's understanding of climate issues, the effectiveness of their approach toward climate-related risks, and their readiness to capitalize on new opportunities. Many companies use their compliance with TCFD to stake their claim to climate change leadership, including BlackRock,[26] Moody's,[27] and Citi.[28]

These two frameworks provide excellent guides for a company starting on its climate journey. Both publish extensive technical notes containing a wealth of useful information, such as the nuances of carbon footprint calculations, acceptable third-party verification mechanisms, and specific ways to engage with customers, suppliers, policy makers, and other stakeholders. CDP, following its commitment to transparency in assigning grades to companies' responses, publishes a painstakingly detailed scoring guide. This provides a valuable opportunity for your company to "optimize" your answers by focusing on the information that carries the most weight in determining your grade. It also makes you privy to the intentions behind climate reporting and the direction society at large expects companies to take on their climate policies.

That said, while both CDP and TCFD can serve as excellent resources, they are too complex and inaccessible for smaller companies to rely on. The Fortune 500 may have the resources to hire an army of consultants or to allocate tens of millions of dollars for this type of broad reprioritization and reorganization, but most companies do not. To be successful on a global scale, climate action needs more than a handful of flagship innovators driving it. Every company, big or small, needs clear, applicable tools to develop a comprehensive, actionable plan for its next steps around climate and sustainability. This book will show you how to do just that.

## Come Together

Before your company can take on this challenge, you first must overcome a long-standing tradition of 20th-century environmentalism: the rhetoric of "us versus them." On one side of this tradition, there are anticorporate activists, ranging from Greenpeace to the extremes of eco-terrorist groups. On the other side, there are antienvironmentalists who lobby against environmental protections and snub the "tree huggers." This polarized narrative has cast businesses in a variety of negative roles—from vile opportunists to outright villains.

This characterization, while unfair, contains some truth. Corporations have put more effort toward hampering climate action than supporting it. According to the Union of Concerned Scientists, between 2002 and 2010, of the 28 largest U.S. companies publicly engaged on climate matters, 19 had their "anti-climate" political activities outweigh their "pro-climate" engagement.[29] In a 2019 report, InfluenceMap found the largest oil producers collectively spent over $200 million lobbying *against* U.S. climate regulations.[30] Some companies fan the flames of climate denial, as Exxon did for decades, even while their own scientists sounded the alarm on climate change.[31] Some engage in blatant greenwashing, such as Nestle Waters Canada's 2008 claim that "bottled water is the most environmentally responsible consumer product in the world" or BP's 2019 global ad campaign focused on clean energy, despite only 3 percent of their revenues coming from such sources.[32]

This corporate malfeasance has begun to catch up with the worst offenders. In spring 2021, The Hague's Court of First Instance found Royal Dutch Shell partially responsible for climate change and ordered the oil company to reduce its emissions by 45 percent by 2030. The plaintiffs in the case were the Dutch branch of Friends of the Earth, 6 other organizations, and 17,000 citizens who demanded that the court order the polluting multinational to emit less $CO_2$ to save the climate. The organization called the judge's ruling "a historic victory."[33]

At the same time, the court did not specify how Shell should implement its decision or how the court would monitor its compliance. Shell had already updated its plan to reduce its GHG emissions in February 2021, just months before the judgment came out. Their new plan was to reduce carbon dioxide emissions by 20 percent by 2030, 45 percent by 2035, and 100 percent by 2050. This clearly wasn't fast enough for the judge, who insisted on aligning the emission-reduction goal with the Paris Accord, resulting in a more aggressive timeline. Given that the Paris Accord was signed by countries' governments rather than private enterprises, and technically, Shell's original plan did not contradict national laws and regulations, it seems unlikely that the judge's decision can be enforced.[34] But the very fact of the decision should warn other companies to be aware of just how much pressure they could face.

Given the tumultuous history between corporations, nature, and society at large, environmental activists have had good reason to cast business leaders as villains. At the same time, most businesspeople approach their work with the best of intentions and have an understandable tendency to push back against the environmentalists' charges, especially since the environmentalist point of view has its own set of faults, as well. Despite its noble cause, the environmental movement has tended to assume its leaders are capable of vocalizing the unspoken needs of future generations and nature itself. They often adopt a technocratic attitude and often show little regard for the people whose entire livelihoods will be destroyed in a decarbonization effort. At times, this attitude borders on outright contempt for less educated populations. With the rhetoric of "us versus them" reigning supreme, many environmental organizations and experts treat companies and large segments of the public as disposable adversaries. They make rare exceptions for a few poster children of climate action, typically in industries that are relatively easy to decarbonize, such as the CDP's

"A-listers," including HP, Estee Lauder, CVS Health, Moody's, Intel, Ecolab, Patagonia, and U.S. Bank.[35]

The anthropogenic origin of climate change makes it easy to get stuck in a never-ending cycle of blame. Yet, conversation about who is to blame distracts from conversations about how we might fix it. In the words of author and historian Valerio Massimo Manfredi, "There are no simple answers to complex problems."[36] Making corporations or environmentalists out as the enemy is a simple answer, and it's wrong. The only real enemy is climate change itself. The global, complex nature of climate change requires that we capitalize on the shared genius of humanity. As Julian Simon shows in his seminal book, *The Ultimate Resource*,[37] human ingenuity is the only truly limited resource. We must shift the paradigm away from "us versus them" toward simply "us." Consumers, regulators, environmentalists, and corporations must come together.

Solving the climate conundrum will require an unprecedented degree of cooperation, particularly within the private sector. Time and again, the private sector has developed solutions to global issues. In the face of the COVID-19 pandemic, a few large companies developed and rolled out vaccines in record time. We must provide the same response to climate change. This fight will require new GHG emission-reduction technologies, drastic improvements in energy efficiency, near-total de-carbonification, carbon sequestration, and perhaps even climate engineering. These innovations will require mainstream acceptance, significant capital investment, operational spending, and consumer interest and support. Only a concerted effort from the private sector, in full partnership with the government and the public, can deliver it.

On some level, the public knows that mitigating climate change will depend on companies like yours. Despite the legacy of "us versus them," the public recognizes the power of business as a tool for driving the sort of broad societal change the climate crisis requires. As noted by public communications experts Victoria Esser and Graeme Trayner, "While Americans do not generally trust businesses' intentions, they do trust businesses' capabilities, certainly more than they trust those of governments."[38] CDP's 2015 Carbon Majors report found that 100 companies have been responsible for over 70 percent of global GHG emissions since 1988.[39] Had they included smaller organizations, this number would likely be nearer to 100 percent. You have an opportunity to make a massive impact, and the public trusts you to make it. So yes, "Tag, you *are* it."

## Climate Action That Counts

Think, for a moment, about all the departments in a business that are connected to climate change. The operations and supply chain departments emit carbon by shipping and sourcing. Manufacturing emits, and plants often face risks from severe weather events. The finance, accounting, and compliance teams have to deal with financial penalties for climate inaction or failure to report. The PR and marketing teams need to publicize climate action or handle bad publicity resulting from inaction. Employee health and safety departments have to keep workers healthy while facing higher temperatures and emergent diseases. I could go on—the point is that climate change touches every part of an organization.

And yet, many companies still keep their sustainability teams siloed and lack the authority necessary to impact all the varied areas across organizations that need to be at the table to truly address climate change. Almost all of my clients have started out doing this. Several of them employed Chief Sustainability Officers with a fancy title, but these officers felt frustrated and disempowered to affect corporate strategy. Or, as in the case of several energy companies I have worked with, the sustainability team might not even have a C-level role, and, instead, is left to languish in the depths of some other department (most commonly, investor relations, communications and marketing, supply chain functions, or environmental health and safety).

When companies do create these separate sustainability offices, they do it with the best of intentions. They want to show the public that they are serious about combating climate change and so they dedicate sizable funding to the office and give it a highly visible position. But this is a mistake. All it does is create an unnecessary silo and an office that lacks the necessary power to execute its mandate. The gap between stated climate goals and their action grows. Initiatives sputter, and climate concerns never receive the attention they demand.

The first step, then, toward climate readiness is to empower the people you have working on the environment. That means you will need to enable a broad-based Sustainability or Environmental, Social, and Governance (ESG) function with the authority to guide climate strategy, drive the execution of climate-related initiatives, and ensure that the corporate strategy and climate strategy stay aligned. My experience suggests that this function should be matrixed into the very heart of the business. The Sustainability or ESG function should report to the group with the highest possible vantage point so they can access and understand the nuances of the overall corporate strategy, as well as the actions of each department. Ideally, this would mean that the Sustainability team reports directly to the board, but if that's not possible, then reporting directly to the strategy or finance leadership should also work. For example, our fertilizer producer client has placed climate management under Finance, allowing for greater transparency, coordination and accountability in integrating climate readiness across the organization. Wherever this team ends up, the key is to make sure its leadership has authority. Because climate change impacts every part of a business, the people working on climate strategy need to have access to and the ability to provide input on every aspect of the business.

A lot of companies hesitate to create such an empowered sustainability office because they fear that a focus on climate strategy will hurt their bottom line. Fortunately, climate action can grow profits. When companies act in concert with climate-focused governmental policy, entire markets shift. For example, the European Union has developed robust practices of energy-saving and GHG reduction. Since 2005, the bloc's GDP has increased without an increase in final energy consumption.[40] The rising tide of climate risks and regulations is also a rising tide of business opportunity: the opportunity to make your operations more efficient, enter new markets, reconfigure your supply chains and logistics, or introduce new products. Your company needs to be ready to capture its fair share of the $100 trillion "pie" of potential investment in decarbonization technologies, as well as the myriad opportunities that come with your company helping the world adapt to the changing climate.[41]

On a more personal level, this book might just help you maintain your personal bottom line, which is to say, your job. Research shows that "CEOs are significantly more likely to be fired when risk exposure to ESG issues reaches extreme levels."[42] Like the fertilizer producer at this chapter's opening, you will soon face (if you haven't already) stakeholder demands for a strategy that integrates climate into all aspects of your organization, regardless of your size, sector, or geography. Rising to this challenge requires that you engage all stakeholders, from your lowest-paid employee to your biggest investor, and examine your operations with climate in mind. Instead of letting the caprices of stakeholders, governments, and the environment pull you in a million different directions, take this opportunity to step back and appreciate the big picture of how climate and your company intertwine.

There is no easy path to adapting to climate change, but in the chapters that follow, I will simplify this transformation into a series of accessible, actionable steps. This book will enable you to see what risks are real and what are merely a mirage, and how to become a resilient leader who can respond to any coming crisis.

# CHAPTER 2

# Reduce Your Footprint

Any climate strategy starts with measuring your organization's carbon footprint. That's the total amount of greenhouse gases (GHGs) —primarily carbon dioxide ($CO_2$) and other pollutants like methane ($CH_4$) and nitrous oxide ($N_2O$)—that are generated directly or indirectly through your operations along the entire value chain. Carbon footprint is usually measured in units of carbon dioxide equivalent ($CO_2e$, where "e" stands for "equivalent"). The reason we convert everything into $CO_2e$ is so that we compare apples with apples in terms of how much your emissions contribute to climate change. You see, all greenhouse gases are not created equal. They have different levels of global warming potential (GWP). That is a measure of the heat-trapping ability of a greenhouse gas over a specific time horizon, typically 20, 100, or 500 years. GWP is expressed as a factor relative to carbon dioxide ($CO_2$), which is assigned a GWP of 1. For example, methane ($CH_4$) has a higher GWP than $CO_2$ because it is more effective at trapping heat in the short term. Its GWP is around 28–36 over a 100-year period. Nitrous oxide ($N_2O$) has an even higher GWP, with a value of about 265–298 over a 100-year period.

Now, the corporate carbon footprint takes into account everything—from the energy a company uses in its day-to-day operations, such as energy consumption, transportation, industrial processes, and waste generation, to the emissions produced when its fleet of vehicles hits the road. We're talking about the direct hits (like burning fossil fuels for heating or powering the company's facilities) and indirect ones (the pollution created during the production of cutting-edge equipment the company has its eye on). And, as we will discuss in Chapter 3, your company's carbon footprint includes emissions generated up and down your value chain. It's our way of saying, "Hey, everything we do has an impact on climate, and we've got the receipts!"

For most companies, it starts with carbon dioxide, which is the primary by-product of burning fossil fuels. From the late 1700s to 2019, the concentration of $CO_2$ gas in the earth's atmosphere rose 46 percent.[1] According to the Intergovernmental Panel on Climate Change (IPCC), the steep rise in $CO_2$ concentration is the main driver behind climate change.[2] By now, many organizations—especially large ones—have gained awareness of their carbon footprint and taken action to reduce their emissions. Smaller companies have been following suit.

While admirable, these initial steps seldom go far enough. True climate readiness requires a fundamental shift in a company's view on greenhouse gases. Instead of treating them as an afterthought, companies must consider the impact *any* decision will have on their emissions. This will not only dramatically reduce a company's carbon footprint but also its future costs. Governments, investors, and lending institutions will continue to punish reckless emitters with higher taxes, interest rates, and fines. Lower emissions will also foster consumer goodwill and have the potential to drive higher sales.

It takes three steps to bring about this shift: measuring your carbon footprint, setting clear and realistic carbon reduction goals, and setting an internal price for carbon.

## Measure Your Footprint

To grasp and tackle your company's carbon footprint, you will have to consider multiple sources of greenhouse gas emissions that it generates. These sources are grouped into Scopes 1, 2, and 3. Here's a breakdown: Scope 1 deals with direct emissions stemming from what the company owns or controls, like vehicles and buildings. Scope 2 focuses on indirect emissions resulting from purchased electricity, steam, heating, and cooling. Scope 3 captures all other indirect emissions across the company's value chain, spanning areas such as business travel, procurement, waste, distribution, and even energy consumption and emissions associated with consumer use. This is a very broad set of activities, and while specific categories of Scope 3 emissions can vary slightly between organizations and industries, the 15 categories defined by the Greenhouse Gas Protocol are the ones most commonly used.[3]

I recommend, at a minimum, that every company track its total GHG emissions, its emissions per unit of production, and per full-time employee. That way, you will have a sense of not only your total (or "absolute" emissions) but also the carbon intensity of your operations. Small businesses can start by using a free online calculator, such as the one developed by CoolClimate Network at the University of California, Berkeley.[4] For larger companies, Greenhouse Gas Protocol is a great resource for detailed methodologies and guidance on developing a comprehensive inventory of your emissions,[5] and countless online tools simplify the process and visualize the output.

Your first step in assessing your company's carbon footprint is to define boundaries for the assessment. In simple terms, the boundary of a carbon footprint assessment defines the limits of what you will consider when measuring the environmental impact of a product, service, or organization. It's like drawing a line around everything that contributes to greenhouse gas emissions. This boundary helps us see the full picture of where emissions come from, including things a company directly controls, like its buildings and vehicles, and things that are indirectly linked, such as the energy used to make the products it sells or the travel associated with its business. You need to understand this boundary to accurately gauge and manage your company's overall impact on the environment. When figuring out the boundaries for a carbon footprint, companies typically choose one of the two main methods: operational control and financial control.

Operational control boils down to what a company directly manages. It includes emissions from stuff a company owns or has a tight grip on—think factories, company cars, and the energy their use generates. However, if something's not directly in the company's grip, like leased spaces or jobs it outsources, those emissions might be excluded from the carbon footprint calculation. This means that under operational control rules, Scope 3 emissions may be excluded. Picture

---

[*] Co-developed by the World Resources Institute (WRI) and the World Business Council for Sustainable Development (WBCSD), Greenhouse Gas Protocol is a set of international standards for measuring and reporting greenhouse gas emissions.

a manufacturing company factoring in emissions from its factories and delivery trucks, excluding emissions from leased office spaces.

Financial control looks at the money game. It ropes in emissions from activities where a company's got some skin in the game, financially speaking. If a company has a solid financial stake, like joint ventures or investments, it brings those emissions to the carbon footprint party. Even if a company doesn't hold the reins on day-to-day operations, if it's got some serious financial interest, those emissions are on the books. Imagine a company with a piece of the pie in a joint venture—it would tally up the emissions from that gig in its carbon footprint, even if it's not pulling the strings day in and day out.

Companies can and do change the boundary of their carbon footprint assessment over time. Adjusting the boundary often reflects an evolving understanding of environmental impact or changes in business operations. If your company is growing, you may have to adjust your carbon footprint assessment to account for emissions associated with its expanding operations. This includes acquisitions as well as organic growth. As your company establishes offices in new regions, you might need to consider the unique energy profiles and environmental factors of each location to provide a more accurate assessment. Regardless of the reason for the change, you must make sure to provide a clear justification for this decision and document it thoroughly.

Gathering data for your carbon footprint will differ depending on the scope. For Scope 1, get the scoop on fuel use in company vehicles, heating systems, and equipment. Dive into fuel bills, meter readings, and other operations-related data. Scope 2 data will come from utility bills, which you will use to determine how much electricity, steam, or cooling your operation is consuming. And for Scope 3, cast a wide net: collect data from suppliers, track business travel mileage, scrutinize waste streams, and take a look at how your employees commute.

When you have your data together, it's time to crunch some numbers. Use well-known emission factors—you can get them from reliable sources like the GHG Protocol or national databases. Convert your collected data into carbon equivalent emissions using these factors. If you've got specifics, great—use them. But if not, default values will do the trick. Remember, emission factors and what your company's up to can change, so keep your inventory up to date. This ensures accuracy and shows your true carbon footprint. Now, let's look at some real-world examples.

Take emission factors, for instance. What you may use in China for electricity might not match up with what's used in the United States. That's because energy sources and technologies vary. For example, when evaluating GHG emissions from agriculture, different European countries might use different emission factors—it all depends on farming practices and land use. Transportation emissions in India could differ from those in Canada, thanks to diverse vehicle fleets and fuel types. It's all about the specifics.

Now, about data quality. In places like Germany, data on industrial processes might be top-notch due to advanced monitoring. But in some developing countries, it might not be as stellar. In a similar way, when considering land-use changes, accurate data might be a bit trickier to come by in some developing countries compared with those with easy access to satellite monitoring. Complicating the picture are methodological updates. Different countries might adopt the latest guidelines at different speeds. So, estimating emissions across countries where you have operations might not sync perfectly.

Policies and regulations will impact your calculation, too. For example, the United States and Norway might have different reporting rules for the oil and gas sector because, you guessed it, their national regulations aren't the same. Each country might have its own standards for calculating emissions based on its policies. Plus, national policies on carbon pricing or taxation can shake things up, influencing how industries report their emissions.

Sector differences add another layer of complexity. For example, think about the textile industry—the way emissions are assessed might be totally different between countries with different production processes. Calculating emissions from coal mining can also vary based on the mix of mining methods and energy use. Even emissions from aviation might not be apples to apples, thanks to differences in aircraft fleets, flight patterns, and fuel types across countries. The better you are at considering all such factors when calculating your company's carbon footprint, the closer you will get to the true picture of its impact.

Wasn't it a blast going through all those calculations? The good news is, there is software that can churn out results faster than you can say "carbon footprint." The bad news? Remember the "garbage in–garbage out" rule? It still holds. You've got to understand, at least on a basic level, how these calculations work to confidently handle the software—or at least give the results a nod of approval. What are the perks of implementing this software? It's not just about getting to numbers quickly. It can also make life easier by simplifying data collection. Oh, and did I mention it could slash the costs tied to data collection and reporting? Some software solutions out there can help you develop a strategy to cut down your carbon footprint, assess risks and opportunities linked to climate change, report your climate-related activities to CDP (formerly known as Climate Disclosure Project), and keep an eye on your monitoring and data collection system. So, think of it as your climate superhero—crunching numbers, saving costs, and making you look good in the eyes of the climate-conscious world.

Digital solutions for calculating greenhouse gas emissions—both separate and additional modules of enterprise resource planning systems—have many players in the game. You've got new products popping up from existing software bigwigs, startups making their mark in the field, and collaborations with service providers. Names such as Optera, Microsoft, Salesforce, Wolters Kluwer Enablon, UL Solutions, Velocity EHS, Benchmark Gensuite, and SAP are in the mix. Although the scene for carbon reporting and management software is getting crowded, no single vendor covers all the bases. It's a dynamic field with various players, each bringing something different to the table.[6]

When selecting a software solution, keep an eye on the features that truly matter to your organization. Look for robust functionality in data acquisition and aggregation for Scope 1, Scope 2, and Scope 3 data. Even if all you are using to track your carbon footprint is an Excel file requiring manual data collection and entry, make sure you can retrace your steps and document all assumptions. Your climate data will more than likely originate from diverse sources, some less apparent than others. The data may reside in disparate systems. But no matter what, your information should come from the general accounting data to ensure a seamless connection to this single "source of truth."

To streamline carbon disclosure management, any solution you choose should not only handle numeric data but also accommodate non-numeric information, such as organizational data and program descriptions. It should also facilitate a seamless workflow, allowing for multiple reviews and approvals, especially by and from the executive team, along with easy edits. And throughout the entire process, you should prioritize data quality control, ensuring accuracy at every step— you will thank yourself come audit time.

Beyond the basics of accounting and reporting, a comprehensive carbon reporting and management solution might include modules for planning and executing greenhouse gas emission reductions. It could also support setting and managing net-zero targets, along with overseeing the intricacies of carbon credits. So, when you're on the hunt for software, think about these functionalities to ensure it meets your needs across the board.

## Put a Price on Carbon

Why take an interest in the nitty-gritty of carbon accounting, you ask? Well, those numbers aren't just digits; they can translate into actual cash and influence your overall financial picture. This is where carbon pricing—a game-changer that attaches a monetary value to the carbon emissions you generate—steps in. It's like putting a price tag on your carbon footprint.

Carbon pricing can take a couple of different forms: One is a carbon tax, where you pay a set amount for each unit of carbon you emit, and the other is a cap-and-trade system, where there's a limit (cap) on overall emissions, and companies can buy and sell (trade) allowances to stay within that limit. In either case, the idea is to create a financial incentive for cutting down on emissions. Carbon pricing mechanisms are dynamic, and prices can change over time based on market conditions and changes in policy.

Real-world instances of carbon pricing include, for example, the emissions trading system (EU ETS) in the European Union, which is a cap-and-trade setup where companies trade allowances, and prices dance to the tune of market supply and demand. Recently, these prices have been swinging between approximately €50 and €100 per ton of $CO_2$.[7] Meanwhile, the United Kingdom plays a different game with its carbon price floor, setting a minimum price for carbon emissions in the power sector.[8] Switzerland has its own emission trading system, echoing the EU ETS approach, with prices ranging from 10 to 80 per Swiss Francs ton of $CO_2$.[9] Norway has a carbon tax, while Sweden has both a carbon tax on fossil fuels while also joining the EU ETS system for covered sectors. Carbon emissions are certainly no longer free.

In the United States, there isn't a nationwide policy for carbon pricing, but various states are taking matters into their own hands. One standout is California with its cap-and-trade program designed to put the brakes on greenhouse gas emissions from major industries, such as electric power plants, electricity imports, and large industrial plants. On the East Coast, a group of northeastern states, including Connecticut, Delaware, and others, teamed up for the Regional Greenhouse Gas Initiative (RGGI) targeting power plants. Covering 11 states representing over 20 percent of the U.S. population, RGGI is considered one of the world's most effective cap-and-trade programs. Since its 2009 launch, RGGI has led to a 45 percent decline in $CO_2$ emissions from the power sector in participating states and is now on a path to achieve a 70 percent reduction in emissions by 2030 compared with 2005 levels.[10] Inspired by these examples, Washington and Oregon have been exploring their own versions of cap-and-trade regulations, while Hawaii has been looking at implementing a carbon offset program, aiming at creating a marketplace for investing in carbon reduction projects.

If you are not dealing with regulator-imposed payments for carbon emissions, it still makes sense to set an internal price of carbon for use within your company. Businesspeople are trained to make decisions based on numbers. They look at what an investment will cost and what they think the return might be, and they choose whether to move forward. This methodology works to make money, but in a climate context, it fails horribly because companies seldom know how to calculate the cost of their environmental impact. Building a new plant might cause 400 metric tons of $CO_2$ emissions, but nobody would ever know, and they would have no way of determining how much that might *cost*. When you put an internal price on carbon emissions, leaders gain an easy way to factor climate considerations into their strategic and decision-making process.

The practice is not new. Some sectors—such as oil and gas, minerals and mining, and electric utilities—have been using internal carbon pricing since the 1990s.[11,12] Today, companies use an internal price of carbon to achieve emission reduction goals, preemptively address stakeholder concerns, lay their claim to social impact leadership, and prepare for future policies that restrict carbon emissions. For example, Danone reports its carbon-adjusted earnings per share (EPS) using an internal carbon price of €35 per metric ton of GHG, which showcases the company's success in reducing its carbon intensity (i.e., the amount of GHG emitted per unit of product).[13]

There are several ways to set an internal price of carbon. For example, companies that operate in a jurisdiction with carbon taxes can set the internal price at the actual price they pay. Some companies establish a price based on governmental regulations they foresee on the horizon, while others set their price with a specific goal in mind, such as a net-zero commitment or a science-based emission reduction target, which will be described in further in this chapter. To do this, they turn to third-party guidance to determine their pricing. For example, the high-level commission on carbon prices estimated that companies should set internal carbon prices between $40 and $80 per metric ton in 2020 and between $50 and $100 by 2030 to reduce their GHG emissions in a way that would comply with the requirements of the Paris Accord.[14]

Some companies that don't face external penalties for carbon use their internal price to set up an internal system of penalties and encentives. For example, if you set a price of $80 per metric ton and undertake a project that "weighs" 300 metric tons when adding up emissions from the use of raw materials, logistics, and energy, then you would divide $24,000 to emissions-reducing investments. The choice of the methodology is ultimately yours, and it will depend on your climate ambitions and resources. If nothing else, you could look at existing carbon penalties in other jurisdictions and set your internal cost of carbon at the same level. Either way, when used consistently in the corporate decision-making process, adding a dollar sign to your carbon emissions will result in a more accurate accounting and better planning for contingencies related to climate.

Setting an internal price on carbon will allow you to weave climate responsibility into the very fabric of financial planning, business strategy, and investment decisions. It's becoming a must-do, especially with tightening regulations and carbon taxation on the horizon, pushing companies to take climate considerations seriously. As the European Union tightens regulations, countries are aligning their policies to meet these standards, making internal carbon pricing a vital tool for businesses navigating this evolving landscape.

## Decarbonization Levers

Measuring your company's carbon footprint is great, but measurement alone does not constitute a strategy. The next step for your organization involves the development of a comprehensive strategy to manage and reduce your carbon footprint, also referred to as a decarbonization strategy. Decarbonization involves reducing or eliminating carbon dioxide and other greenhouse gas emissions from your value chain.

From a report by a research firm Verdantix, it's clear that companies are gearing up to spend significant amounts of money on decarbonization in the coming years. But it's not just about money; your challenge involves untangling and decarbonizing core business processes.[15] There are emerging best practices, commonly known as "decarbonization levers," that can serve as valuable sources of ideas and inspiration from others who've been there. The good news is that you're not alone in this. Companies all over the place, from different industries, are on the same journey.

*Energy Efficiency Improvements*

Improving energy efficiency is a key strategy for companies looking to reduce carbon footprints while boosting operational efficiencies and savings. Some efficiencies are clear, no-brainer type ones like, for example, replacing all lighting with LEDs. I have seen it work for businesses ranging from large manufacturing facilities, to massive real estate and logistics operations, to small professional services offices, and to hotel chains. For example, according to Oliver Winter, the CEO of a&o hotels, their investment in LEDs was recouped within a year.

For less obvious improvements, you may need to conduct energy audits to pinpoint and rectify areas of energy waste. Upgrading machinery to more energy-efficient models will be the carbon footprint reduction panacea for some companies. This is particularly relevant to industries centered around significant built assets like education, health care, or real estate; the pathway to decarbonization involves retrofitting and enhancing building efficiency. This not only aligns with environmental goals but also proves economically beneficial. Enhancements in building systems—such as upgrading lighting, heating, ventilation and air conditioning (HVAC), weatherization, or boiler tune-ups—can naturally lead to reduced energy consumption. It's a win-win situation where environmental gains come hand in hand with cost savings. Additionally, local utilities may offer incentives to building owners and managers to implement energy-efficient measures, further sweetening the deal.

On the flip side, non compliance with regulations, like the per-square-foot fines under New York LL97,[16] can pose financial risks. Investing in improving buildings' environmental performance is not just an eco-friendly choice but a strategic move to avoid potential costs associated with non compliance. The long-term benefits, both in terms of sustainability and financial prudence, make such investments worthwhile.

### Process Optimization

Another way to reduce your carbon footprint may involve changing your processes. While technically sophisticated, these strategies are becoming more commonplace. For example, in the manufacturing sector, companies are increasingly leveraging advanced analytics and sensors to keep a close eye on their production lines. Take an automobile manufacturer, for example, which might utilize sensors to keep tabs on energy usage. By employing advanced analytics, they can pinpoint bottlenecks, ultimately fine-tuning the entire production process and cutting down on waste.

On another front, real estate firms are delving into the realm of sensors and analytics through building management systems. With these, they can actively monitor and regulate the conditions within their buildings. Armed with data-driven insights, adjustments to heating, ventilation, and lighting systems become more precise, leading to reduced energy consumption and a lighter environmental footprint.

### Renewable Energy

Renewable energy sources, such as wind, solar, and hydropower, have become increasingly cost-effective, rivaling traditional fossil fuels.[17] Countless companies are opting to power their offices, warehouses, manufacturing facilities, and data centers with renewable energy sources, steering away from traditional fossil fuels. In sectors like media and telecom, and especially technology, there's a notable push to adopt renewables and integrate carbon capture technologies. This can also be an option for industries with exceptionally high and tough-to-cut energy requirements, such as chemicals, metals, and mining.

One way to make it happen is to invest in on-site renewable energy sources, such as solar panels or wind turbines. Or, you can enter into power purchase agreements (PPAs) with providers of renewable power who will design, install, and operate a solar energy system to ensure clean energy at a set rate for years in advance.[18] Explore community solar or shared renewable energy programs. If you decide to take this route, you will be in good company: For example, Google has invested over $3.5 billion in large-scale renewable energy projects[19] and PPAs to fulfill its pledge of operating on 100 percent renewable energy.

The overhead costs connected to PPAs—and the capital outlay and operating costs of on-site renewables- can be staggering. As an alternative, you can purchase renewable energy credits (RECs), which essentially allow you to subsidize the environmental benefits associated with a certain amount of renewable energy production. Renewable energy providers and developers often offer RECs as part of their services, and online marketplaces specialize in facilitating REC transactions. Environmental organizations, utilities, and energy brokers, as well as government programs, may also provide opportunities for companies to buy RECs. Certification programs, such as Green-e, verify and certify the legitimacy of RECs. Just make sure to do your due diligence on the seller and understand the specific terms of the RECs.

Start by exploring the various programs and incentives offered by your local utility company. Many utilities have initiatives to encourage businesses like yours to embrace renewable energy. These initiatives include financial incentives, technical support, and special rates for using renewable energy. By looking into these options, you can make smart choices that may reduce the financial impact of adopting renewable energy solutions.

For instance, consider "green rate" programs. Your company could choose a higher percentage of renewable energy for its electricity supply, aligning your operations with cleaner and more sustainable power sources. Duke Energy, covering multiple states in the United States, offers solar rebates to commercial customers, making it more affordable to install solar panels.[20] REC programs may allow your companies to support renewable energy without making significant infrastructure changes.

## Fuel Switching

Many industries deeply tied to fossil fuels—such as automotive, aviation, freight, oil and gas, and plastics—are now making a shift toward cleaner energy sources. This transition, known as fuel switching, is essentially about moving away from traditional fossil fuels to options that contribute less to carbon emissions.

One scenario is the natural gas to propane conversion, which can help companies reduce their carbon footprint.[21] This decision could stem from factors such as cost considerations or the increased availability of propane. Another potential move is the coal to natural gas conversion, typically used by power plants or industrial facilities seeking to lower emissions and improve operational efficiency. The shift to natural gas is favored for its cleaner combustion compared with coal.

In the transportation sector, conversion from diesel to compressed natural gas is gaining traction. Simultaneously, some maritime vessels or industrial boilers are making the transition from heavy fuel oil to lighter petroleum fuels.[22] Additionally, biomass or biogas utilization represents a move toward renewable sources, with facilities adopting biomass or biogas for heating or power generation, often derived from organic materials such as wood, agricultural residues, or waste.[23] The hydrogen economy[24] shows promise for sectors that are challenging to electrify, complemented by the innovative approach of bioenergy with carbon capture and storage.[25] There is much experimentation across industries adopting alternative fuels tailored to specific contexts. This shift is motivated by compliance with environmental regulations and an overarching goal to minimize climate impact.

### Waste Reduction and Circular Economy Practices

In your quest to reduce your company's carbon footprint, adopting circular economy principles can be a powerful strategy. This involves minimizing waste generation by implementing recycling programs for materials, such as paper, plastic, and electronics. Beyond this, companies explore changes in product design to make recycling or repurposing more straightforward. One impactful move is the shift from traditional packaging materials to eco-friendly alternatives, such as recycled paper and biodegradable packaging, contributing significantly to the reduction of carbon emissions.

Companies like IKEA are at the forefront of this movement, actively working toward a circular economy by designing products that prioritize recyclability.[26] IKEA's commitment aims not only to cut down on waste but also to encourage the reuse and recycling of materials. In the electronics sector, Dell has been making progress with its circular economy initiatives, focusing specifically on recycling and repurposing electronic waste.[27] This approach directly aligns with reducing the environmental impact of electronic products. Similarly, H&M has taken a stand in the fashion industry by committing to a circular fashion economy.[28] Over the years, the company has been backing textile collection and recycling initiatives taking on the challenging task of creating a circular textiles value chain and reducing the environmental footprint associated with fast fashion. These are large companies with deep pockets, but opportunities to lead the circularity movement are available to companies of all sizes.

### Transportation Decarbonization

One impactful way for companies to actively reduce their carbon footprint is by transitioning to a low-emission or electric vehicle fleet. This move not only lowers emissions but also aligns with the global push toward sustainable transportation. Encouraging telecommuting and flexible work schedules further contributes to emission reduction, addressing the environmental impact of daily commuting. Additionally, optimizing transportation routes to minimize fuel consumption is a strategic step that positively impacts a company's overall carbon emissions. Noteworthy examples in this domain include Nissan, a pioneer in electric vehicles, with its popular model, the Nissan Leaf. Nissan's commitment to electrification is a tangible effort to curtail emissions in the transportation sector. Similarly, Volkswagen, with its significant shift toward electric vehicles, invests in both technology and infrastructure to actively decrease the carbon footprint associated with its transportation products.

Another innovative approach is exemplified by Ridepanda,[29] a startup addressing climate issues by prompting companies to reassess their practices regarding benefits and carbon footprint. This startup shifted from a direct-to-consumer model to a corporate focus in 2020, finding success particularly with technology companies, those with sustainability goals, city governments, law firms, and even hospitals. A notable example is a hospital in Portland, Oregon, that has a seven-year waitlist for parking spots, showcasing the growing interest in and need for carbon-conscious transportation solutions. Ridepanda's broad approach underscores its adaptability, illustrating how corporate thinking can shift to not only reduce carbon emissions but also extract tangible benefits from embracing sustainable transportation practices.

## Carbon Capture and Utilization

Carbon capture and utilization (CCU) stands out as a promising strategy for curbing carbon footprints, particularly in industries grappling with substantial emissions and where traditional mitigation approaches face challenges. Take the power generation sector, for instance. Power plants, especially those relying on fossil fuels, emit large amounts of carbon dioxide. CCU technologies emerge as a game-changer by capturing and reusing these emissions, preventing them from contributing to atmospheric pollution. Notably, coal-fired power plants can implement CCU to capture carbon dioxide emissions, offering a tangible contribution to the overarching goal of emission reduction. As CCU continues to evolve, its application in diverse sectors, including the chemical industry and the bioenergy-agriculture nexus, showcases its potential to not only reduce carbon footprints but also to foster economic and environmental benefits.

In heavy industries, such as cement, steel, and chemical production, CCU becomes a beacon of hope. Cement production, notorious for its significant carbon footprint, can leverage CCU to capture and repurpose carbon dioxide emissions generated during manufacturing processes. Similarly, the oil and gas sector, notorious for releasing carbon dioxide during extraction and processing, can employ CCU technologies to mitigate environmental impacts. Oil refineries, for instance, can capture and repurpose carbon emissions produced during the refining process, signaling a more sustainable trajectory for the industry. For example, Chevron is working on carbon capture initiatives to reduce emissions from its operations. The company is exploring ways to capture carbon dioxide from industrial processes and power generation.[30]

When captured carbon dioxide cannot be reused, it must be securely stored to prevent its release into the atmosphere. This is called carbon sequestration. Examples of carbon sequestration technologies include geological storage, when carbon dioxide is injected into an underground saline aquifer, and direct air capture, with companies like Climeworks[31] capturing carbon dioxide directly from the air for storage or industrial use. There are even ocean-based storage experiments and mineralization.

These cutting-edge technologies, while promising, are also expensive. But, luckily, nature already does a great job of sequestering carbon through plants and soils. Trees absorb $CO_2$ as they grow, storing it in their biomass. Healthy soils also hold onto carbon effectively. Getting involved in forestation projects can be a more accessible way for companies to contribute to increasing carbon storage.

### Carbon Offsetting

Somewhere along the line, each company hits a point when cutting carbon emissions is no longer feasible. When that happens, investing in carbon offset projects is like giving back to the planet for the unavoidable emissions. These projects can be about planting trees, supporting clean energy, or capturing methane to balance out your company's impact.

If you're interested in buying carbon offsets, you will likely have to go through a third-party provider. There are many out there, so it's important to research and choose a reputable one that offers high-quality offsets. Offsetting your carbon footprint is a bit like doing a puzzle—you want projects that are legitimate and make a real difference. So, pick projects certified under standards like the Verified Carbon Standard or the Gold Standard.[32] You can buy offsets from specialized online platforms like Terrapass, Carbonfund.org, Cool Effect, or South Pole. Some forestry companies offer carbon offset programs tied to their tree planting and conservation initiatives. Several environmental nonprofit organizations offer carbon offset programs focused on specific areas like renewable energy or energy efficiency projects. Other players include offset brokers, financial institutions, and project developers.

When you're building your offset portfolio, you can put all your resources into projects of the same type—or mix it up. The only rule is that offsetting should be the final touch not the main show. Offset wisely, and let your company's commitment to sustainability shine through.

## Bringing It Together

Navigating the landscape of carbon footprint reduction is no stroll in the park. There are lots of options, and more are on the horizon as technologies mature. You've got to tailor your approach based on your industry. I have pointed out key industries for each decarbonization lever, but realistically, you are going to be looking at a full "menu" of options. This is especially true if your emissions are all over the place, which is the case in many industries, including agriculture, retail, tourism, waste, or wholesale trade. The key is to diversify—and thoroughly document—your efforts to mitigate your company's climate impact.

Some items on your "menu" of decarbonization options may look half-baked. Despite the rapid growth in technologies, some have not yet reached the commercial scale necessary to offer accessible options to companies like yours. But, with the right economics, such options are bound to appear. You just need to stay abreast of the developments while capitalizing on other—typically more behavior-focused—trends like reduced routine business travel postpandemic.

Your success in reducing your company's carbon footprint hinges on emphasizing return on investment and crafting compelling business cases. For example, timing energy efficiency upgrades to existing asset replacement schedules may make massive capital investments more feasible—and more palatable for the company's leadership. You need to be creative in thinking through all possible options and transparent in acknowledging potential implementation challenges.

Every change requires a supportive organizational culture. Your success in achieving decarbonization goals will depend on your ability to foster collaboration across the entire company. You need everyone in sync, from the ground up to the big shots in the boardroom.

Cross-functional teamwork is the secret sauce for making your grand eco-friendly plans actually work.

## Set Clear and Realistic Carbon Goals

In an attempt to position themselves as climate leaders, many companies have set bold carbon goals. Some, such as Microsoft, commit to removing *all* the carbon that they have ever emitted from the environment, thus going "carbon-negative."[33] A much more common and only slightly less bold commitment is to achieve "net-zero" emissions. In other words, companies promise to remove or offset as much carbon as they produce each year. Between 2019 and 2020, the number of businesses setting net-zero commitments tripled from around 500 to 1,541[34] and continued to grow ever since.

These are both noble goals, but, as always, the devil is in the details. Companies are notorious for making net-zero commitments without disclosing their carbon reduction strategies.[35] Granted, the nondisclosing companies may not have crafted a plan yet, but they intend to. Or they might simply be trying to cash in on the good public relations (PR) their commitment generated, without making the investment necessary to achieve carbon neutrality. In all likelihood, the gap between commitment and action represents a mix of both factors. Regardless of the reason, when companies commit to a goal without a plan, the ones that fail to act set themselves up for failure. When they inevitably fall short, they open themselves up to criticism and charges of greenwashing that could flip the initial PR bump into a proper PR beatdown. This is, of course, in addition to the missed opportunities to help the environment.

The first step is to determine what goals are realistic. The net-zero option requires an immense investment and a complete transformation of every part of a business. In most cases, even these changes won't result in net-zero carbon emissions. Too much of the contemporary global economy relies on carbon, and each company can only do so much to reduce its footprint. To reach net-zero emissions, almost every company will have to buy carbon offsets, which essentially credit an organization (or individual) for subsidizing carbon reductions (e.g., by paying for a new wind turbine) or creating a carbon sink (e.g., restoring parts of the Amazon rainforest). A commitment to remove all previously emitted carbon from the air—such as Microsoft's—requires an even greater investment in carbon offsets.

If this seems feasible for your company, then great, go for it. Just make sure to consult and comply with the existing guidance articulated by the International Standards Organization[36] and the UN-sponsored high-level expert group on the Net-Zero Emissions Commitments of Non-State Entities. In a nutshell, if you take this seriously, you are required to establish short-term, medium-term, and long-term absolute emissions reduction targets, along with relative emissions reduction goals across the entire value chain. These should align with the latest IPCC net-zero greenhouse gas emission pathways, limiting warming to 1.5°C, and aim for a global emissions decline of at least 50 percent below 2020 levels by 2030, ultimately reaching net-zero $CO_2$ emissions by 2050, followed by achieving net-zero greenhouse gas emissions shortly thereafter.[37]

Unfortunately, most companies lack the resources to achieve net zero, much less a commitment similar to Microsoft's. In those cases, I recommend using science-based targets (SBTs) to set a climate agenda. Originally designed by The Science-Based Targets Initiative (SBTi), SBTs look at an organization's current emissions relative to those of the rest of the world. Then, they calculate how much that company would need to cut its emissions in order to do its part in meeting the minimum of the Paris Climate Accord.

This approach has several benefits. First, it allows you to position your company as a climate leader in a way that is directly tied to shaping and driving the ultimate outcomes of low-carbon transition. In your announcement, you can say, "We have done the analysis and determined that this is what we need to do and can do right now. If every other company did the same, we could keep total global warming under 1.5°C." Second, SBTs move you closer to climate readiness because they require you to audit your current climate situation. In other words, instead of a knee-jerk, poorly considered net-zero pledge, which requires little effort to declare yet has a serious chance of going unfulfilled, an

SBT forces you to examine your broader business strategy to determine how much you emit and where you rely on carbon. For some companies, SBTs are more achievable than net-zero commitments. Others can be challenged by SBTi's restriction on the use of carbon offsets. So, it is OK to wait to adopt these goals. Before publicly committing to these goals, you need to have a sense of what is realistic for your company to achieve.

If you choose to set SBTs, SBTi's website[38] provides a defined set of steps, including expert review and approval. There, you can find detailed guides to conduct a necessary analysis as well as guidance specifically tailored to different sectors.

Despite the complexity, SBTs are not just for giant companies with deep pockets. At the beginning of 2025, over 7,000 companies had committed to setting SBTs, and over 1,500 have set net-zero commitments.[39] These numbers continue to grow. For small companies, expert consensus is that it "depends on ambition." So this is basically up to you. In addition to demonstrating ambition, it is a way to engage in a meaningful conversation around your company's impact on climate. In any case, regardless of which goals you set, make sure you support them with an actionable, realistic decarbonization plan.

# CHAPTER 3

# Think Life Cycle

No business exists in a vacuum. Today, the value chain for each product—a term used by business and climate experts to describe the full, cradle-to-grave life cycle of a product or a service[*]—touches more parts of the world than ever before. Multinational organizations often source raw materials from one country, build component parts in multiple other countries, assemble their product in yet another country, and then distribute it around the world. Even that covers only a product's first half of life—the customers then use and (eventually) dispose of the product, which may be dispersed to various places across the globe.

For years, multinational corporations have claimed ignorance about their suppliers' and customers' behavior and impotence in their ability to influence them. Increasingly, regulators and the public don't accept these excuses. Eventually, you will have to account for the full life cycle of your product: If you start now, you can get ahead of the regulations and gain a competitive edge over any who lag behind. At the same time, you can create a positive environmental impact and capitalize on the PR bump that it brings. In addition to pulling the decarbonization levers, we discussed in Chapter 2, transforming your products' or services' full life cycle adds two key steps: assessing the life cycle and engaging with suppliers and customers.

---

[*] The definition of value chain used by CDP differs from the commonly accepted definition that includes only those activities by the company necessary to deliver the product to consumers. CDP's definition also includes "downstream" activities on the consumer side, using the product and disposing of waste. Throughout this chapter, I will be using the more accurate term "life cycle."

## The Value of Life Cycle Assessment

To reduce your company's carbon impact, you first need to understand its full extent. Think about everything that has to happen before your company gets to do anything—extracting and processing raw materials and transporting them to your site. Then, you get to do your magic—making a product. After that, usage, retail, and waste disposal come. And suppose all you do is provide a service. In that case, you are still dependent on any supplies and consumables—and responsible for corresponding waste, including such less-obvious things like emissions generated through work from home or the use of third-party cloud services.

Understanding this entire process can help you assess the climate-related consequences of your choices and work toward minimizing harm at each stage. To do this, I recommend conducting the life cycle assessment (LCA). LCAs measure just how much water, energy, and other materials each step in the production process consumes and how much carbon and waste each step produces. Fundamentally, an LCA offers a framework to measure the complete carbon footprint of a product or service. It can also offer insights into the impact successful climate mitigation actions can have on your company's reputation. An accurate LCA reveals which climate interventions will make the greatest impact. Then, when you go to intervene, you can use the LCA to prove the necessity of your requests from suppliers and customers.

Conducting thorough LCAs can be integral to your overall climate readiness approach in three ways. First, this process will train employees to consider all the economic and environmental factors in their decision making and search for ways to reduce the company's environmental impact. For example, LCAs can help manufacturing companies determine which equipment to install and involve scrutinizing carbon emissions, which is especially critical for items with extended replacement cycles. And they would be in good company. Companies like Toyota use LCAs to assess the environmental impact of their vehicles from raw material extraction to end-of-life disposal.[1] Patagonia is known for using LCA to analyze the environmental impact of their apparel. This helps them make more sustainable material and production choices.[2] BASF, a chemical company, integrates LCA to evaluate the sustainability of its products and processes, aiming for reduced environmental impact.[3] From food and consumer products to building materials and construction processes, conducting an LCA can be truly enlightening.

Second, life cycle analysis can act as a predictor of future regulations and how they will affect business. Already, regulatory bodies around the world utilize LCAs in their decision making and policy-making processes. For example, The European Union (EU) has adopted the product environmental footprint (PEF) method, which is based on LCA principles, to assess the environmental impact of products and services.[4] This information is used to develop eco-design regulations and inform consumer labeling schemes. For instance, the EU's Ecodesign Directive[5] requires manufacturers to provide consumers with information on the environmental performance of their products, including energy consumption and greenhouse gas emissions. This information is often based on LCA studies. California turned to LCAs to understand just how much carbon certain biofuels produced over their lifetime and used their findings to set biofuel policies. This information was used to develop the state's low carbon fuel standard, which requires fuel producers to reduce the carbon intensity of their fuels.[6] By conducting LCAs, you will be able to stay ahead of the curve on regulatory developments.

Finally, holding your company to LCA standards helps you prove (and brag about) the sustainability of your products/services to customers, investors, climate reporting services, and regulators. For example, in its guidance documents, CDP encourages companies to use LCA as a tool for gathering data and developing their responses. The CDP questionnaires contain questions about life cycle emissions and value chain impacts including upstream and downstream activities, such as resource use, emissions, and waste generation. In addition, LCAs can also safeguard your marketing against greenwashing claims by backing up your climate-friendly claims with real evidence.

But it's not just about talking the talk. LCAs help companies not only walk the walk toward being genuinely green but also become more efficient—and profitable—at their core. This is not just about climate. An LCA can provide important keys to understanding your costs, which is important for planning, monitoring, and evaluating business results. The popularity of lean manufacturing is pushing more companies to embrace LCAs to unearth problems, mitigate risks, and pinpoint avenues for profit and expansion. Your efforts can enhance financial analysis and material flow tracking, ensuring consistent reporting that makes sense to international data aggregators and ranking agencies and which can help spot discrepancies early on. You will also beef up your internal audit and quality assurance processes, adding more variables to the mix. Carbon footprint LCAs offer a fresh perspective on data aggregation, demanding a deep understanding and precise handling of existing processes and material flows.

As you can see, LCA can be valuable to various folks within your company. For those in product management or research and development, it could be a go-to for keeping up with regulations and developing new eco-friendly products. Supply chain management teams will find it useful for spotting top-notch suppliers and checking out their climate credentials. Marketing and sales professionals will appreciate it for meeting customer calls for sustainability, making your company's brand shine brighter. And for those in the executive suite, LCA helps weave sustainability into every nook and cranny of the business, keeping things in-line with the planet-saving agenda.

## Conducting a Life Cycle Assessment

Conducting an LCA involves four main steps. First, you define the goal and scope of the assessment, setting the purpose and boundaries. Begin by focusing on a specific product and determining the functional unit for evaluation. It's vital to clearly define the system boundaries of the assessment, detailing which life cycle stages are included and excluded. For example, deciding whether to count certain Scope 3 emissions,[†] like those from employee commuting or product life cycle, can differ depending on national reporting rules. Differences in how we draw the

---

[†] See Chapter 2 for a discussion of Scope 2 and Scope 3 emissions.

line between Scope 2 and Scope 3 emissions could impact how we assess indirect emissions related to energy use.

Next, identify the system for assessment. This involves defining the product life cycle and selecting impact categories for analysis. For example, if your goal is to produce an environmental product declaration,[‡] you must ensure alignment with standards set by regulators. It's important to be clear about what aspects you won't be assessing to streamline your analysis. For example, you may choose to exclude deep dives into certain portions of the value chain or acknowledge that social implications may not significantly impact your evaluation.

Then, gather detailed data on raw materials, energy use, and emissions throughout the product's life cycle. Ok, when I say "detailed," let's be realistic. In the beginning, your data may be woefully incomplete. This is OK. Start where you are, document your assumptions, and work to clarify matters as you go. Don't wait for researchers to come up with precise parameters—when something is missing, make assumptions. Your ability to make timely decisions will often be more important here than precision. This step is commonly referred to as the life cycle inventory. Next comes the evaluation of the environmental impact across various categories, providing insights into the product's overall footprint. The methodology is very similar to assessing your company's carbon footprint described in Chapter 2, but the reporting boundaries will differ. You will still assess direct, energy, and other indirect emissions within each site's specific production systems. This means setting clear rules and specific measurements for what goes in (such as raw materials, materials, and energy) and what comes out (such as products and greenhouse gases). Then, you will analyze the data for each product's creation process and estimate the emissions they generate. Your info will come from tracking what materials and energy are used for making each product. Then, use flow charts to see how materials move around and how emissions happen during product creation. Using such flow models will help your team avoid confusion and capture important context.

---

‡ Environmental product declarations are common when following guidelines from ISO 14025:2006. Environmental Labels and Declarations.

Finally, you need to analyze the findings based on the uncovered data. After gaining insights, you will need to draw conclusions on emissions, compare products, and identify opportunities for impact reduction. These steps together form a structured process to thoroughly understand a product's environmental implications from start to finish. ISO 14044:2006[7] published by the International Organization for Standardization guides this process.

Each step of this process requires not only a commitment to getting it right but also some high-octane analytical skills. Navigating the ISO standards associated with them can be challenging. The life cycle inventory phase of LCA, in particular, can be complex, involving time-consuming data collection. This is why LCAs are usually conducted by trained professionals—and this is where involving outside consultants may be the best choice for your organization. Hire them to stay updated on trends and handle complex technical matters. But involve them only in specific areas like addressing material flow issues. Keep a tight grip on your data and the entire calculation process to ensure future ease of use and usability.

Software solutions like environmental intelligence platform by Ecochain[8] allow broader accessibility—and tighter control over your data. In essence, they offer an activity-based footprinting approach for comprehensive company and product-level LCAs. Data, often sourced from bills, are collected through sheets at company, process, and product levels, supplemented by questionnaires and industry averages. Unlike traditional LCAs conducted by external consultants, Ecochain's approach allows dynamic updates as aspects of the chain change, providing more ongoing and actionable insights for companies implementing recommendations.

To conduct a proper LCA, you need input from various departments such as production, engineering, and, of course, finance. Everyone has a role to play in this process, and this will be the case regardless of whether you hire consultants or do it yourself. Much of the data will come from financial reporting—think all the expenses involved in making products or providing services and keeping the lights on, including buying materials and shipping them around, dealing with the waste that comes out, spending on green tech, and keeping systems that reduce environmental impacts up and running. Financial professionals may not grasp the full scope of operations, meaning that all these data must be put in the right context by professionals across your organization. For example, in working with the fertilizer producer client, much helpful information came from the company's dedicated personnel responsible for certification and documentation of products for sale in various markets, particularly for exportation. These folks already know the ins and outs of how products are used and go the extra mile to meet customer demands. In this case, they offered different-colored fertilizers for various markets based on cultural preferences. These people knew exactly how to interpret and use data for the back end of our LCA.

Implementing the ISO standard for LCAs to the letter might not be feasible on the first pass. This process involves extensive research considering regional differences, cultural factors, and operational processes. Realistically, assumptions, such as using general agricultural research data instead of specific product information, will need to be made. Even though we're making estimates for all emissions, using spend-based or global industry averages instead of supplier-specific and location-specific emission factors can lead to some seriously inaccurate estimates. Over time, you can work to develop more precise estimates, with suppliers playing a defining role in providing accurate data for each product. Most important, you want to avoid getting mired in the technicalities of the ISO standard and instead prioritize a practical, action-focused approach.

It all begins with high-quality data, so make sure you're getting it from trustworthy and representative sources for everything that goes in and comes out. Being upfront about how you're crunching the numbers and where the info's coming from is important too, so you will want to document everything really well to make sure folks can check it out and trust what we're saying.

Here's a final word of caution: This won't be a walk in the park. According to Deloitte's research, Scope 3 emissions pose a challenge for almost all companies. The trickiest areas to measure include the end-of-life treatment of sold products, with 45 percent of companies finding this tough, followed by fuel- and energy-related activities not covered in Scope 1 or Scope 2, which 40 percent struggle with. The CDP reports that Scope 3 emissions usually make up 75 percent of a company's GHG emissions, but for certain industries like financial services and capital goods, it can be close to 100 percent. For sectors heavily reliant on raw materials such as real estate, construction, metals and mining, and agriculture commodities, Scope 3 encompasses 90 to 95 percent of the company's value chain. Many organizations face challenges in collecting detailed primary data from their suppliers, often resorting to secondary data like industry averages or spend-based emission factors. So, don't judge yourself too harshly: any response from suppliers is a step in the right direction toward understanding your entire carbon footprint.

## Don't Go It Alone

Once you've got a handle on how your products impact each stage of their life cycle, you can start taking action to shrink that impact. Suppliers and consumers are your key allies in this effort. I recommend pulling your ideas together in a value chain engagement plan, which covers everything from getting raw materials and supplies to making the product, selling it, and providing after-sales service. The main goal here is to tackle greenhouse gas emissions all along the value chain, gathering the data needed to guide corporate decisions and influence major suppliers and consumers to cut down on emissions.

This plan should mesh with your company's overall business strategy, its procurement policy, and environmental (or sustainability) policy. Your procurement policy may already prioritize environmentally friendly suppliers, but it should also include climate criteria for picking and evaluating suppliers. Your environmental policy should commit to climate action and outline expectations of environmental responsibility from supply chain partners. Finally, while your company's overall strategic focus is on growing sales in key markets, it should also address the climate side of things.

In some cases, bringing greater transparency to supply chains in search of climate impacts could alert you to unrelated yet pernicious issues, such as conflict minerals, modern slavery, or other potential issues or controversies. Addressing carbon footprint concerns can help preempt them.

### Engaging With Suppliers

When you engage with suppliers, your ultimate goal is to get them to change their behavior. After all, this is all about reducing the carbon footprint of your company's supply chain. But first, you need to understand their impact on your company's overall carbon footprint. For that, you need to implement a system to track greenhouse gas emissions from suppliers. Initially, this can be nothing more than an Excel spreadsheet, which is as fine a place to start as any. The quality of the data going in will likely be low, so think of this as more of a process—and an opportunity for continuous improvement. For example, one of our clients, despite historically being quite selective about which suppliers it teamed up with based on their ecological and social responsibility, discovered a big gap in how they tracked greenhouse gas emissions. When they asked raw material suppliers about their emissions, almost three-quarters either couldn't provide any info or didn't have it, demonstrating that there's a serious lack of data out there. And over 60 percent didn't even bother to respond. Your results may be better—or worse—depending on your market, your mix of suppliers, and the dynamics of your relationships. Either way, you will likely discover that there is room for improvement.

To prompt positive changes in supplier behavior, you will also need to take proactive steps by raising awareness about the importance of addressing climate change and reducing greenhouse gas emissions. You are in a unique position of incentivizing innovation to drive market change. But be careful. No business leader wants to feel forced to adopt a change. For that reason, do everything possible to partner with your suppliers instead of strong-arming them. Consider how you might work together to find more climate-friendly ways to conduct business and even offer to share some of the financial burden. Educate them on why you're taking the steps you are taking, and demonstrate how they can benefit from decarbonization. Or, offer incentives to decarbonize. For example, in 2018, Walmart rolled out Project Gigaton, a commitment to cut 50 million metric tons of GHG emissions from its China supply chain by 2030. As part of the program, they offered "preferred supplier status"—essentially preferential treatment and more contracts—to any supplier that committed to reducing its carbon footprints.[9]

Collaboration with suppliers can take different forms within the same industry—and it's up to you to develop engagement programs with your own unique flair. For example, Danone, a food and beverage giant, extends its efforts into promoting sustainable agriculture. The company teams up with farmers to push for regenerative farming methods and cut down on the environmental footprint of their supply chain.[10] Unilever uses its Sustainable Agriculture Code to help farmers adopt eco-friendly practices.[11] Mining conglomerate BHP, recognizing its outsized impact on the maritime shipping industry, has formed a consortium with Rio Tinto, Oldendorff, Star Bulk, and the Global Maritime Forum to support the development of an iron ore maritime "green corridor," fueled by green ammonia.[12]

Eventually, you will want to integrate your climate goals with your supplier selection processes, too. This will ensure that climate readiness remains a core focus in your relationships with suppliers, reinforcing your commitment to reducing your carbon footprint across the entire supply chain. When you're picking suppliers, make sure your criteria cover a few key things. First off, check if they've got published reports on greenhouse gas emissions, including any national frameworks or international ones like CDP. You'll also want to know if they've got strategic plans in place for dealing with climate issues, such as setting targets for cutting emissions and taking action to make it happen. And, last but not least, you can ask them to provide data on their actual greenhouse gas emissions, both direct and indirect, per unit of whatever they're supplying, all measured in metric tons of $CO_2$ equivalent.

Once you start receiving data, you can decide on how you will use it along with other supplier selection criteria. For example, one-fifth of Vodafone's supplier selection criteria since 2020 has been linked to its commitments to carbon reduction as well as its principles of circular economy, diversity and inclusion, and health and safety policies.[13] In April 2021, Salesforce rolled out its new supplier contracts which require its vendors to set carbon reduction goals and deliver products and services on a carbon-neutral basis.[14] Some of our clients have gone further by providing financial incentives to suppliers who demonstrate significant progress in reducing operational emissions (Scopes 1 and 2) or emissions both upstream and downstream in the value chain (Scope 3), further aligning their practices with sustainability goals.

It's typical for big companies to source raw materials, fuel, goods, and services from a slew of suppliers all over the globe. As supply chain managers organize and run tenders, they typically strive to make procurement processes more efficient and transparent, ensure a level playing field for all potential suppliers, maintain consistent requirements, and evaluate proposals objectively. While procurement procedures do consider the eco-friendliness of materials and resources, greenhouse gas emissions aren't factored in. Yet supply chain emissions can pack a punch, especially in industries like manufacturing, energy, transportation, construction, or agriculture. Suppliers of raw materials (like purchased goods and services), fuel (those fuel and energy activities not covered in Scope 1 or Scope 2), and transportation services (transportation up the value chain) tend to rack up the highest emissions. When you are ready to tackle them, go after categories with the largest spend first.

If you have a smaller business, you do not have to make climate-informed supplier selection as complex or as far-reaching as some of the larger companies. A simple first step is to adopt and publish a supplier climate or sustainability policy to underscore the importance of climate performance to your company. Request that your suppliers provide information on their carbon footprints. Then, think about how you will use this information in making your contracting decisions. When all other factors are equal, will those who provide information have a leg up? Will you be willing to award contracts to higher bidders demonstrating superior climate performance? Whatever way you decide to go, make sure to keep your supplier selection policies transparent and open. This maintains your suppliers' and consumers' trust and reinforces the shared benefits of your policies.

Now, for a shot of realism, let me quote Oliver Winter, the CEO of a&o Hostels, with 39 properties in 25 cities in 9 countries, the largest privately owned hostel chain in Europe: "What helped our mission, … the biggest push we had was the energy crisis we had the last 12 months. That was where even our suppliers woke up and listened when we said, could you make it more energy efficient?" The energy crisis of late 2022 prompted a&o Hostels to reconsider the industry-wide practice of bringing laundry from Berlin-based hotels to Poland, 200 km away, to capitalize on cheap labor. Turning to local laundry suppliers, a&o built relationships with existing local establishments eager to collaborate on making their processes more climate-friendly. a&o worked with these laundry facilities to help them switch electricity and heating suppliers and reduce the temperature of washes, thereby reducing their own carbon footprint. This, of course, was in addition to massive reductions in carbon emissions as they were no longer trucking loads of laundry back and forth through international borders.

You have to be opportunistic. Ultimately, you are expanding your responsibility over the parts of the value chain over which you have no direct control. It is not simple or easy. But if done right, it will be well worth it.

### Engaging With Customers

Customers are the lifeblood of your company. They can be loyal or fickle. They can be prone to following fads. Yet they can also be deeply committed providing the momentum for societal and environmental change in the absence of regulations. By engaging customers creatively, you can empower them to become active participants in reducing the carbon footprint of your products.

First and foremost, make information easily accessible and digestible. This means labeling products with carbon footprint data, including tips on how to minimize carbon emissions during use, and providing clear instructions on what to do with products once they've reached the end of their life cycle. Whether through blog posts, videos, or social media campaigns, sharing information about a product's sustainability features and suggesting actions users can take to make a difference will go a long way. Running targeted campaigns and events is another great way to spread the word. Whether these are in-person or online, focusing on how to use products in an eco-friendly way, how to maintain them, and how to make repairs can make a big impact.

You may want to use incentives and gamification to make sustainable choices feel rewarding and fun to your customers. One way to do this is by offering perks, such as discounts, loyalty points, or badges, to folks who use products in an energy-efficient way or bring them back for refurbishing. Another approach is to set up challenges and competitions to get people excited about shrinking their carbon footprint. By offering rewards for hitting environmental targets, you can turn sustainability into a friendly competition. And don't underestimate the power of gamification. Adding features to products that track and score users' energy savings or resource efficiency can make sustainable choices more engaging and motivating. Even Starbucks is getting in on the action, offering a discount and bonus stars to customers who bring their own cups.[15]

As you think about your product's entire life cycle, consider designing for energy efficiency in the first place. You can integrate features that save energy in your products and make customers aware of the benefits for their bottom line as well. Offering repair and upgrade options can encourage customers to hang onto their products for a longer period of time—and make your revenue more predictable and customers more loyal. To address the last step in the product's life cycle, think about developing take-back and recycling programs. Patagonia takes this approach by offering a lifetime warranty and repair services for their clothing. Their Worn Wear program allows customers trade in or buy used clothing.[16] The LEGO Group focuses on keeping those iconic bricks in the game through their circular economy efforts. Their brick take-back program, REPLAY, has already handled a staggering 200 million bricks in the United States and Canada, and it's gearing up for a launch in the UK.[17] And don't forget about supporting community projects. Investing in local initiatives that directly tackle carbon reduction or environmental restoration shows your commitment to making a positive impact where it matters most.

The best way to engage customers is to devise climate-friendly ways to use and dispose of products, then make it easy for customers to apply these methods. Take, for example, Nespresso, which sells machines that extract espresso shots from single-use aluminum pods. Aluminum is easy to recycle, but because the pods contain coffee grounds, many recycling facilities do not accept them. To reduce their environmental impact, Nespresso devised and distributed a free tool that allowed customers to easily and safely cut open their used pods, empty the grounds into a composting bag (also provided by Nespresso), and then recycle the pod.[18]

You do not need to have the global reach of Nespresso to offer your customers a creative, impactful business model to help them reach their climate goals. For example, SCRAP NYC serves a wide range of potential customers—from individuals cleaning out their closets to global hotel chains looking for ways to responsibly discard sheets and towels at the end of their useful life. Yet, all of them lack convenient ways to dispose of used textiles in an environmentally responsible way. Although the notion of circularity in fashion has been around for a while, scalable, profitable operations are still elusive because they tend to focus on a single link in a chain and fail to close the loop of serving the needs of those who donate clothing or textiles. By focusing on addressing the initial, most challenging customer-facing element of circularity, SCRAP NYC has been able to build an entire ecosystem of recyclers, retailers, resellers, and other partners to help its customers reduce their carbon footprint in an easy and satisfying way.

As you expand into new markets, you will also need to ramp up information and education efforts and spark innovation among consumers. For example, our fertilizer producer client supplies fertilizers to more than a hundred countries in Asia, Europe, Africa, South America, and North America. To maintain and build its market presence, the company pulls at all stops—by communicating with consumers, providing its own agronomic services, partnering with research institutions, developing new solutions that meet market needs, participating in industry exhibitions, holding its own events for consumers, and developing product eco-labels.

Your decarbonization plans will have the greatest likelihood of success if they take into account the interests of your suppliers and consumers. Find ways to help a supplier's bottom line or ease the strain on a customer's wallet. And be consistent. Once you set a carbon reduction goal for your product's life cycle, stick to it and remain on message. Transformation takes time, so provide your suppliers and customers with opportunities to evolve and grow in partnership with you.

# CHAPTER 4

# Understand and Manage Climate Risks

When our team first met with the leaders of the fertilizer company mentioned in Chapter 1, those executives were already feeling the impact of climate change. Everyone, even the old-timers who were initially hesitant to acknowledge the reality of climate change, could tell. They'd seen thawing permafrost and rapid freezing and thawing that damaged infrastructure. What was in store for the company as a result of the future impacts of climate change would be much worse—increased precipitation, higher winds, and more destructive natural phenomena, such as more frequent flooding and fires ignited by lightning. Any or all of these threatened to ratchet up their costs and create operational nightmares. Even when they didn't feel the impact directly, when prompted to consider the changing climate, they saw potential disaster wherever they looked: underground pumping stations that could be waterlogged, landslides that could overwhelm sludge collectors and tailing pits, containment dams that could be breached, gas pipelines that could break, cranes and other equipment on the verge of becoming unstable, employees prone to accidents and illness, and regulatory action impending. Potential threats to profitability were everywhere.

In the face of such dangers, they felt helpless at first and just tried their best to ignore it. This reluctance to act came, in part, because they had internalized much of the mainstream climate change rhetoric, which paints a picture of climate change that will rapidly lead to a world that resembles something from a *Mad Max* movie. In that world, most people die, and those who live suffer from debilitating illnesses and punishing food and water scarcity. Early in the climate movement, this rhetoric was intended to convince reluctant business and political leaders to take climate change seriously. However, the apocalyptic rhetoric causes an instinctive rejection by those overwhelmed by what seems like impending doom.

Many companies, in the face of such a prognosis and considering remaining uncertainty surrounding the exact impacts of climate change on the ground,[1] rightfully reason that they wouldn't do anything except carry on and hope that disaster wouldn't completely upend their operations. The "apocalyptic" climate rhetoric makes them believe that their only choice was to prepare to shut down their operations in a not-so-distant future. This resulted in a situation in which it was easy for the company's leadership to simply avoid the topic of climate for some time. This approach is a massive mistake. While a single company can't undo climate change, it can—and must—prepare for its impact, from environmental conditions to accelerated regulatory developments. The key is to stop denying the potential of a disaster and start managing risk.

According to Rich Sorkin, CEO of Jupiter Intelligence, a climate analytics firm, "in 10 years, there won't be a large entity anywhere on the planet that does not have a handle on its climate risk. Consumers, shareholders, and employees won't stand for it."[2] In addition, companies will not be able to tolerate indefinitely the increasing threats to their profitability or loss of market positioning due to climate regulations.

## From Uncertainty and Inaction to Managing Risk

While changes in Earth's climate are nothing new under the sun, the change we are about to experience—the change to a significant degree caused by human activity—is indeed new. New enough that most companies have neither any idea how to handle it nor know what specific impacts they should prepare for and the likelihood of such impacts. From manufacturing to real estate, in my experience, companies have limited—if any—understanding of how climate change will impact their businesses or of how to mitigate the impact. Absent this information, they treat it as pure uncertainty which leads to inaction.

The critical first step in any company's journey toward climate readiness is shaking off the "uncertainty paralysis." Instead of uncertainty, consider potential climate impacts—even those that are unknown

—as risks. When you treat something as a risk, you can apply economic and scientific models to determine the probability that something will happen and the impact it will have if it does. In this case, the fertilizer company ran the numbers and discovered that the impacts of increased temperatures could result in a roughly 15 percent reduction in revenue. If you think about the increased rate of defects and equipment stoppage, this makes sense. The company also estimated the probability of it happening in the short term as "very high." From there, they could take action to manage that risk. Based on estimates by internal experts, they estimated the costs of changing certain processes around cooling and condensation systems for equipment at roughly one-eighth of the total estimated revenue loss. The path forward was clear.

Notice that risk management does not mean risk elimination. In the prior example, the only way to eliminate the risk would be to either reverse climate change or decommission the factory. The first option is impossible or, at the very least, too slow. And the second choice puts you out of business—not a desirable choice for most. But risk management—and risk mitigation—is an appealing proposition.

The fertilizer company, like many large companies, already had a robust risk management system in place. Yet, because they had siloed their sustainability offices from the rest of their operations, those existing systems and mechanisms did not initially include climate risks and could not help them adapt to and ameliorate the effects of climate change. In our work together, we helped them realize that dealing with the new challenge of climate change boiled down to mitigating risk. Working together, we added a new emphasis on climate-based impacts to their current risk assessment and management mechanisms. This allowed them to make the most prudent decisions.

## What Are Climate Risks?

Before you can attempt to predict the future, you need to understand your current company's reality—and its immediate, almost-certain future—and what recent shifts led to it. Climate change is permanent, global, and pervasive—punctuated with melting permafrost, coastal flooding, shrinking island states, deserts replacing farmland and gardens, shrinking glaciers, and increasing water scarcity. Climate change is affecting raw material and production flows, disrupting or fundamentally altering value chains. As a business leader, you may find yourself dealing with water use restrictions stemming from droughts in your region. Or you may be facing more frequent heatwaves or floods directly impacting your company's operations, supply chain, and infrastructure.

But understanding climate change goes beyond just noticing changes in nature—its effects ripple through societal and economic systems. This is why the Task Force on Climate-Related Financial Disclosures (TCFD)[3] breaks down climate risks into categories that help companies navigate this treacherous landscape. The TCFD recommends that organizations consider all four categories of climate risks when assessing their financial exposure to climate change.

### Physical Risks

Physical risks stem from the actual physical impacts of climate change. Extreme weather events, such as floods, storms, droughts, and wildfires, are part of the package when it comes to physical risks. And it's not just about the big bang moments; it also includes chronic impacts, such as sea level rise, water scarcity, and heat stress. Companies need to consider the potential damage to their assets and infrastructure, as well as the possible disruption to operations and supply chains. In a nutshell, grasping the scope of physical risks is essential for businesses seeking to fortify themselves against the tangible impacts of a changing climate.

The physical drivers of climate change encompass changes in natural processes and phenomena that create risks of disrupting business processes and supply chains. These include an uptick in the solar radiation index, an overall increase in annual mean surface air temperatures, and a rise in maximum temperatures along with the duration of hot periods during warmer seasons. Additionally, there's an increase in the amplitude and frequency of sharp temperature fluctuations alongside a rise in average annual precipitation and air humidity levels. There are changes in precipitation patterns, particularly during fall and winter, leading to increased snow cover and a higher incidence of floods. There's a rise in sea levels, alterations in river water content, and increasing strength, frequency, and variability of hurricanes, storms, and other climatic events.

Acute climate risks are like sudden punches, intense but temporary, like floods or heatwaves, while chronic risks are like slow squeezes, building pressure over time, such as rising sea levels or changing precipitation patterns. One disrupts lives and infrastructure in a flash, and the other slowly reshapes landscapes and ecosystems, both posing serious threats but demanding different responses for preparedness and adaptation.

Whether acute or chronic, just like medical conditions, physical climate risks can have dire consequences, forcing shutdowns, disrupting supply chains, ratcheting up energy prices during peak hours, or reducing the availability of raw materials. Changes in climate can also affect the quality of raw materials and inputs that rely on temperature, humidity, and other climate factors. For example, cotton yields and fiber quality can be affected by changes in temperature during the growing season.[4] Changes in weather patterns and rising sea levels can affect tourism destinations and infrastructure. Temperature and humidity fluctuations can affect the properties and durability of materials, such as wood, concrete, or steel. Rising temperatures can impact animal health and productivity, timber production, and even the suitability of grapes for winemaking. Changing rainfall patterns lead to reduced agricultural yields, resulting in increased raw material costs for beverage and consumer goods companies and higher, more volatile food prices for consumers. In addition, as climatic changes compound, we should expect more frequent failures in energy, heat, and water supply systems, increased risk of industrial accidents, and longer periods of routine equipment maintenance—all of which increase companies' capital and operating costs. All of these are in addition to the deterioration of employee health, which can jeopardize your company's success.

### Transition Risks

There is much more to climate risks than perceptible environmental shifts, such as extreme weather events. Climate risks also involve potential economic and financial costs linked to the move toward a low-carbon economy. Unlike the direct hits of physical risks, transition risks come from the changes in policies, technology, and markets that tag along with this shift. It's a whole different ball game, and understanding both sides is key to navigating the complexities of climate change.

Transition risks involve a range of factors, including policy and legal changes, such as carbon taxes and emissions regulations. For example, with the U.S. federal Production Tax Credit for renewable energy and California's push for zero-emission vehicles by 2035, companies might find themselves stuck with "stranded assets," such as coal-powered plants or oil refineries, if carbon taxes make carbon-heavy operations too pricey. Transportation costs will climb as regulations drive up prices of high-carbon fuels, hitting the transportation industry particularly hard, given its hefty reliance on oil. Technological advancements play a part, too—think of renewable energy becoming more affordable than fossil fuels. Shifting consumer preferences, such as a growing demand for sustainable products, also fall under the transition risks category.

Ultimately, transition risks stem from political decisions made internationally and within national and/or subnational jurisdictions(s) aimed at curbing climate change by reducing greenhouse gas emissions and promoting cleaner energy sources to mitigate climate change in the future. Key factors include rising prices for energy sources with negative environmental impacts driven by state regulations encouraging the shift to cleaner energy alternatives. Additionally, increased costs for equipment and materials could result from stricter regulations targeting industries with high climate impact. Compliance expenses may also rise due to government regulations on greenhouse gas emissions in countries importing a company's products. Regulatory measures may restrict the entry of goods with negative climate impacts into national markets, influencing consumer preferences toward environmentally friendly products.

Understanding transition risks is important for any company looking to adapt to changing climate and economic landscapes while preserving its finances, reputation, and market share. Different industries respond differently to climate shifts; for instance, telecom or retail companies, with lower carbon footprints, face less heat from regulators, customers, and investors than do utilities or mining firms. While each company's risk depends on factors like location, clientele, and management actions, sectors like power and transportation, subject to increased regulations and shifts in demand, are at the forefront of transitional climate risks. As climate policies gain momentum and companies feel the heat to go green, we might see some big changes in how key business inputs are made, shipped, and used. These changes could have major—and expanding—ripple effects down the line.

### Liability Risks

Liability risks deal with legal or ethical obligations to compensate for damages and losses resulting from climate change.[5] A prime example is the potential legal claim tied to climate change. Imagine facing lawsuits for climate-related damages such as property damage or health impacts —that falls under liability risks. If this sounds far-fetched, consider *Milieudefensie v. Royal Dutch Shell* (2023), where a Dutch court ordered Shell to reduce its global greenhouse gas emissions by 45 percent by 2030 compared with 2019 levels, marking the first successful attempt to hold a private company legally responsible for its contribution to climate change based on human rights arguments.[6] Or take *Communities Around the World v. BP* (2023), in which residents of multiple nations impacted by BP's oil and gas operations sued the company for human rights violations related to climate change impacts. Another illuminating case is *Citizens' Climate Lobby et al. v. Chevron et al.* (2020), in which several U.S. states and cities are suing major oil companies, claiming they knew about the dangers of climate change and misled the public for decades. So far, climate liability litigation has predominantly and somewhat successfully sought to apply pressure on corporate boards through the litigation system. But the overall legal landscape of climate litigation is still evolving, and this makes outcomes hard to predict.

Legal battles are extreme examples of liability risks. Companies that don't comply with climate regulations face the risk of regulatory fines and penalties. Take the case of Volkswagen back in 2016—it found itself slapped with a hefty U.S. $14.7 billion (£11.5 billion) in civil and criminal penalties in the United States.[7] This came in the aftermath of an emissions cheating scandal,[8] which significantly dimmed the prospects of diesel as a future fuel. Fast forward to today, and you'll notice a major shift in the automotive landscape. Now, most big-shot car companies are putting their money where the future seems to be —electric cars. The Volkswagen fiasco shook things up, prompting a redirection of current and future investment toward electric vehicles. This shift is not just a matter of choice; it's a response to climate change and the push for stricter emission targets. The wheels of change are turning, and drivers of electric cars are steering the way forward for the automotive industry.

Insurance companies are finding that climate change is shaking up the way they assess and price risk from extreme weather. This leads to higher insurance premiums and limits to insurance coverage in affected areas. For example, annual reports by the California Department of Insurance indicate consistent requests for rate increases from different insurance companies, often citing wildfire risk as a reason. State Farm and Allstate, two leading insurers, have stopped offering new homeowners' policies in the state, partly due to wildfire risk and high construction costs.[9] The tragic aftermath of the Los Angeles fires in early 2025 has shown just how much of a financial time bomb this situation was. And it's not just California. Farmers Insurance Group withdrew tens of thousands of policies from Florida in 2023, explicitly stating that more frequent and severe weather events driven by climate change make affordable insurance difficult. Bankers Insurance Company also exited the Florida market entirely in mid-2022, citing rising costs and challenges associated with weather events.[10]

As climate change concerns begin shaping the legal landscape at scale, your company may need to start paying attention to liability risks. That way, you will be prepared for any legal repercussions that can come knocking in the face of climate-related challenges.

### Reputational Risks

Now more than ever, a company's climate-related actions—or inaction—can seriously impact its reputation. Think of it as a ripple effect. Negative public perception can arise from how a company deals with climate issues. This, in turn, could lead to a loss of customers or investors—a big hit for any business. In addition, there's the challenge of attracting and retaining talent when a company's reputation takes a hit in the climate arena. Effectively managing and mitigating reputational risks is key for businesses aiming to maintain a positive image and secure their standing in the eyes of the public, customers, and potential employees.

We live in an uber-connected society full of people with rapidly diminishing attention spans. Social media enable consumers to hold companies accountable for their climate impact. Consumer-facing brands that fail to address climate change issues face potential public outcry and even boycotts from some consumer segments. Failure to address climate can also hurt a company's image with employees. The 2017 Eco Pulse study, an annual survey that gauges consumer spending and behavior, shows that the percentage of people who said they had stopped buying a product based on the environmental reputation of a company jumped to 33 percent from just 11 percent the previous year. In the climate change context, reputational risk can be considered as the probability of profitability loss following a business's activities or positions that the public considers harmful.[11]

## Assess Climate Risk

Now that you know what kinds of risks to look for, you can start by gathering the necessary input data for your climate-related risk assessments. Focus on how climate change factors impact your company's management processes and systems. These should cover everything—from procurement, production planning, and sales to IT management, logistics, HR management, and internal audit. Differentiate the company's processes based on their sensitivity to climatic conditions during implementation. Recognize which parts of your operations are more vulnerable to climate-related factors so that you can later tailor strategies accordingly. Focus on the factors causing the most risk and to which your company is the most vulnerable.

To understand risks related to physical changes in your operating environment, enlist your employees and managers including "process owners" for those processes most affected by climate change to help you get a deep sense of your climate context. For the most part, if climate change impacts your customers' willingness to buy from you or affects your employees' behavior (e.g., increased sick leave due to longer and more extreme heat waves), the frontline managers will notice the shift first. They will also be attuned to changes in the maintenance demands and service lives of your equipment. You will need to tap into this invaluable knowledge continuously to keep abreast of your changing operating environments and markets.

For example, when engaging in conversations about risks with a client that was an oil refinery, we made sure to separately discuss regions where specific production facilities were located. This level of precision helped the company leadership make better decisions as they addressed the risks to their operations. At a manufacturing company, we surveyed the frontline managers and set up a system where they could report any climate-related changes up the line.

Assessing some risks, however, will require complex modeling. For example, another client, an innovative data and analytics startup, has developed software solutions to help companies discover, track, and manage complex weather risks that threaten the availability of water. For players in insurance, agriculture, data center development, beverage and bottling, and other water-dependent industries, such a level of modeling sophistication is a must.

To complete the model, look at historical weather patterns and current trends, as well as the costs to comparable businesses, of disasters such as hurricanes, floods, and tornadoes. This is where prior experience and forward-looking insights will merge. Try to get as many data points as possible, so you can understand what a best, worst, and most-likely case scenario disaster would look like. This will give you a sense of if and when inclement weather will strike in the short term and what it might cost.

For regulation-related risks, on the other hand, trade associations, business think tanks such as The Conference Board, and even law firms are typically good sources of information. You can also review materials from international organizations that outline trends in climate regulation and consider how these regulations align with the company's operations and product usage. Think about how they could impact your company's ability to achieve its strategic goals. Consult with your "process owners" if needed. Expert commentary on major regulatory developments can be a great starting point to guide your thinking. But you still must do much of the thinking yourself.

## Putting a Price Tag on the Unthinkable

Now that you have an understanding of the kinds of climate risks your company faces, you can start "translating" this knowledge into the kind of business language that everyone can understand—dollars and cents. In reality, we are likely talking tens or hundreds of thousands—and potentially millions—of dollars.

First, you need to rank climate risks according to their likelihood and severity. For each risk, you will also need to determine your risk management strategy. Risk management will be addressed in greater detail later in this chapter. But, at this point, you still have to make some key decisions on how you will address each of the risks you have identified. Are you going to invest in infrastructure upgrades like flood defenses or storm-resistant buildings? Will you have to diversify supply chains and asset locations to reduce dependency on particularly vulnerable locations? Will you invest in low-carbon technologies or develop sustainable products and services to meet changing consumer preferences? Will you need to buy additional insurance—and, while we are at it, will your insurance costs increase? Or—as an extreme example of risk avoidance—will you close shop altogether?

You can use those risk rankings to plan out how to deal with the big threats, whether by investing in some backup plans, changing up your strategies, or just being prepared to pivot if things start to go south.

All of those things cost money—and this is exactly what we are looking for here. Some companies take this quantitative modeling seriously and produce complex projections using fancy math to determine how different climate factors might impact things like how much money a company makes or spends or the value of its assets. But this does not have to get too complicated or require loads of data and historical info. You can start with simple, back-of-the-napkin estimates. Don't be too easily impressed by the illusory persuasiveness of complex mathematical models. Your most important data will come from your process owners.

For example, if your company has facilities in areas vulnerable to physical climate threats, and you plan on building or hardening your infrastructure, you can reasonably expect increased capital expenditures. Understanding climate risks specific to your company will help identify management decisions. To calculate their potential financial impact, you will have to rely on assumptions about things like the probability of adverse events, the types and severity of impacts, the various costs of mitigating the impacts, and so on. As always with assumptions, the most important part is documenting them rather than getting them perfectly right. The "cone of uncertainty" will narrow down as you move forward, and your initial calculation could be as simple as a share of the total capital repair and construction funds. You could also take a percentage of your ongoing environmental protection costs, labor protection costs, or maintenance.

This calculation may look different depending on your industry. For example, within the transportation sector, extreme weather events pose a significant challenge by causing damage to transport infrastructure and disrupting established trade routes. This disruption not only translates to increased capital and operating costs for fleet owners dealing with repairs and operational adjustments but also prompts the sector to grapple with the imperative to adapt to evolving technological and logistical demands. As the financial services sector experiences an uptick in extreme weather events, it will increase insurance premiums for policyholders and higher payouts for insurance companies. Extreme weather events in construction and building services result in heightened costs for building owners. This has prompted increased investments in both weather-resistant and energy-efficient building products and services to enhance resilience and sustainability in construction practices. Climate change is causing notable shifts in the regions and yields of various agricultural products. For example, in areas like Brazil and Central America, it's projected that around 80 percent of the land currently suitable for growing Arabica coffee will become unsuitable by 2050. This shift is expected to diminish global coffee supply, consequently leading to increased prices worldwide.[12]

All of the above risks have the potential to affect a company's cost of capital. In 2022, several U.S. coal companies experienced significant drops in their stock prices following announcements of stricter environmental regulations and growing investor concerns about the future of coal.[13] In 2021, major oil and gas companies faced downgrades by credit rating agencies concerned about the long-term viability of their business models in a transitioning energy market. This downgrade resulted in higher interest rates on their future borrowing.[14]

## Project Scenarios of the Future

Once you have a good sense of your current context surrounding existing climate risks, you can begin to project and plan for future risks. The best way to do this is through scenario analysis, an established method for making contingency plans in uncertain conditions. Recognize that there will always be a degree of uncertainty in forecasting future climate scenarios and specific impacts on your business.

As a starting point, I recommend that you consider two main scenarios recommended by the Intergovernmental Panel on Climate Change: one with 4°C warming, and another with a "well below 2°C" or 1.5°C scenario.[15] The two scenarios differ significantly in their impacts on companies. The 4°C scenario describes a global failure to limit climate change, which means more extreme weather, placing companies' infrastructure and logistics at significant risk. In this scenario, your company could need to relocate away from disaster-prone zones, reconfigure its supply chains, and shift focus onto different products or services. The prevalence of physical climate risks (such as new weather patterns or higher sea levels) in this scenario would come with a relatively light regulatory burden, which is the main reason this scenario is one to consider. To get the clearest idea, look for climate models that approximate what weather patterns will look like in the areas where you operate. Adaptation and risk conversations need to always occur on the local level, even for multinational corporations.

The "well below 2°C" or 1.5°C scenario reflects more drastic governmental measures to contain climate change. As a result, your company could be dealing with new or increased carbon taxes, lower emission limits, or rigorous fuel efficiency regulations. Companies likely would need to decarbonize at a rapid rate to keep up with regulations. Consumers would demand more climate-friendly products and might pressure your company into taking a more proactive stance toward reducing its carbon footprint. On the positive side, in this scenario, climate change would be far less severe, and, therefore, you would face fewer physical climate-related risks.

If your company develops its own climate risk analysis modeling, you can work to quantify and plug the above conditions for both scenarios into the model to get a sense of what the future might hold for you. In fact, you may want to add or change parameters in your scenarios if the context in which you do business warrants it. For most companies, however, this information can be used without complex modeling. Work with your company's strategy group, if you have one, and discuss it with the board of directors, C-suite, or key managers. Most importantly, think through how you will respond if any of the expected regulatory or environmental changes become a reality.

Following the TCFD's advice, diving into a climate scenario analysis is a multistep process. First, you have to weave this analysis into your company's big-picture planning and risk management strategies. Then, you start digging into the nitty-gritty of climate risks, looking at everything from market changes to how laws might shift. Once you've got a handle on that, it's scenario time—you're sketching out different climate change scenarios that could hit your business and figuring out how they'd play out. After that, you're assessing how all this could impact your business—both the good and the bad. Then comes the brainstorming session: How do you tackle these risks and opportunities?

It might mean shaking up your plans or getting everyone on board. Last but not least, you're making sure all this analysis gets written up and shared in your strategy documents.

Understanding climate scenarios can be a bit of a puzzle for various reasons. First, many organizations don't have a deep grasp of climate-related issues—it's like navigating uncharted territory. Second, there's the challenge of putting a clear price tag on the financial impacts of these climate-related issues—it's not always straightforward math. Another hurdle is the tendency to zoom in on short-term risks, overlooking the potential curveballs that come your way in the long run. It's like focusing so much on the next step that you forget to look ahead. These complexities make climate scenario analysis a tricky business that requires a careful balancing act to account for both current and future challenges.

## Manage Risks

Once you've sorted all your climate risks, it's time to put all this understanding to work. This is where companies have the same general strategic choices they use in managing other risks.* Obviously, there's the risk avoidance game: shifting away from fossil fuels by focusing on developing renewable energy projects, sidestepping the environmental impact of animal farming by producing plant-based alternatives to meat. Automakers are going full-out on electric vehicles instead of traditional gasoline-powered vehicles to avoid fossil fuel risks. Avoiding reputational risks from unsustainable sourcing practices may look like implementing a hard-nosed supplier responsibility policy.

If you're more of a keeper than a dodger, risk retention might be your style. Set lofty emissions goals and invest in green energy, accepting some residual risk while you work on climate change mitigation. Aggressively slashing your company's carbon footprint will make it easier to tolerate the little risk exposure left. Then there's the good old risk transfer. Here, you will be in a company of big corporate names like Coca-Cola, Amazon, and Apple that buy carbon offsets

---

* ISO 31,000: Risk Management standard provides useful practical guidance on selecting risk management approaches.

to shift emissions responsibilities elsewhere. Depending on your level of ambition, you might explore carbon capture and storage tech to stash away emissions or team up with energy providers to power your operations with renewable energy sources.

Managing climate risks can involve multiple areas within your company. For example, in terms of social and HR risks, it's crucial to integrate climate considerations into such HR policies as recruitment and training. Tackling production risks could involve implementing technological and organizational measures to minimize climate-related impacts on production processes. Many of such measures will be industry-specific. For example, agricultural producers may introduce crop varieties with lower chilling requirements that are capable of maintaining productivity through warmer winters. Managing production risks could involve better cold chain management to ensure that perishable goods such as food and pharmaceuticals are kept at required low temperatures during storage and transportation. In mining, you could be looking to enhance ore mining and transportation processes and ensure the smooth functioning of control equipment and power supply. It's also vital to factor climate change into the design of new construction and renovation projects.

Operational risks should be addressed, too, focusing on preventing disruptions to business processes due to climate change. This might involve measures to prevent transportation failures and shipment delays, as well as minimization of negative impacts on ecosystems while adhering to safety requirements. Regulatory risks call for consistent monitoring and response to new climate-related regulations affecting company operations. Financial risks require ongoing monitoring of and swift responses to changes in interest rates, credit terms, and logistics resulting from climate factors. Finally, managing reputational risks involves maintaining a positive climate image amidst increasing demands from consumers, investors, and government bodies in a competitive market.

Some companies are getting creative with their strategies. Take hedging against carbon prices, for example. Companies use it to protect themselves from future costs tied to carbon pricing rules. It's like having a safety net for your wallet against potential carbon-related expenses down the road. Then there's the move to diversify operations. Think of big players like BP—they're not just sticking to oil and gas anymore. They're branching out into renewable energy, hedging their bets, and reducing their reliance on fossil fuels. It's like broadening your investment portfolio to ride out market ups and downs. And let's not forget about having a backup plan for climate impacts. Companies like Nestlé are prepping for extreme weather or resource shortages by drawing up solid plans to keep things running smoothly no matter what Mother Nature throws their way. These strategies aren't just smart—they're essential for staying ahead in a world where climate risks are becoming more and more real.

As you work on formulating your climate risk management approach, you will notice how intertwined many of the issues are. In a way, it is as if you need to introduce climate risks as a new variable into a system of mathematical equations—with impacts reverberating through the entire system. And it's not always easy. According to Declan O'Sullivan, a climate strategy expert in banking, despite the push for climate change stress testing, with average loans spanning from five to seven years, it is hard for management to keep its focus on the distant future of 2050 as a holistic climate strategy would require. Realistically, attention is directed toward immediate factors like the potential introduction of a carbon tax and the credit standings of sectors directly impacted by climate change. The pressing question arises: Should pricing strategies be adjusted to reflect these climate-related variables? However, there's a complication: Climate considerations haven't solidified as concrete factors in credit assessments, and blanket price increases may face opposition. And, while the average person might plan five to seven years ahead, small businesses often struggle to look beyond the coming year or two.

All of this is not to scare you. Balancing climate risk with practical business decisions remains a complex and evolving task. But every company will have to do it in one way or another. Even if you start factoring climate events into the existing risk management system of your company, you will be ahead of the game. Addressing climate risks is not an area of managerial activity but an integral part of your company's risk-based business management system. Over time, you will develop a clear understanding of how much risk the company is willing to take on in the face of climate-related challenges. It's all about aligning strategies with the company's risk tolerance to make informed and balanced decisions. And remember, a good manager manages risks, while a bad one deals with disasters.

# CHAPTER 5

# Discover
# Climate Opportunities

Climate change is like any other massive shift: It offers countless opportunities. Yet most companies fail to recognize and act on this fact. If they do speak of opportunities, they focus almost solely on actions to combat climate change not on what can be done to help individuals, communities, and other businesses adapt to the changing climatic conditions. In my experience, they keep their focus limited, in part, because they don't want to be accused of profiteering off the misfortunes of others. What most companies fail to realize is that seizing a climate opportunity doesn't just benefit their business; it can help the entire world. Climate adaptation is at least as important as our collective efforts to mitigate the harmful impacts of our activity.

Businesses make a profit by providing value. When a company seizes a climate opportunity, they meet a need that didn't exist before (i.e., investing in new renewable energy installations or selling air conditioners to people in northern Canada), or they do something that used to be impossible to achieve better results for their consumers (i.e., using shorter and cheaper shipping routes in the melted Arctic). In short, businesses have a moral responsibility to look for and take these opportunities because they will help the world adapt. And, of course, they can raise the bottom line.

The key reason for the lack of understanding of climate-related opportunities can be traced back to how TCFD defines "risks" and "opportunities" in the context of climate change. It eschews traditional approaches to risk management that separate "factors" (changes in the environment) from "risks" (the negative impacts of such changes in the context of specific organizations, groups of people, etc.). The key here is that when applied in different contexts, the same factor can have both negative and positive impacts. In the current TCFD guidance, factors underlying physical risks, such as changes in precipitation, rising mean temperatures, increasing sea levels, and so on, are referred to as simply "risks." What could be easily considered a technicality leads to a situation where we are not primed to consider the full range of impacts from the changes in our physical environment.

For example, a worldwide pandemic is a risk to companies in the hospitality industry but a potential opportunity for pharmaceuticals. Changes in the areas of production for certain crops are a risk to farmers dependent on growing them in their area but can bring new opportunities to those in the areas now open for production, provided, of course, that they are able and willing to shift gears quickly.

The now globally shared understanding of physical climate change as "risk" leads to a distorted view of opportunities as limited to only those that arise from actions taken to alleviate risks. It is like taking a derivative of a derivative but pretending that it is the original value. This codifies a common view of climate change as something inherently negative, which is of course true at the societal level. This approach also makes perfect sense emotionally—talking about opportunities created as a result of climate change leads to ethical dilemmas, which no one has any real appetite in facing.

However, it is important for business leaders to have the intellectual honesty to see the entire picture, in which both climate change itself, as well as the actions taken to address it, can become a source of opportunities. This is a time for solutions. While the pressure to act mounts, you need to understand the entire range of opportunities in climate mitigation and climate adaptation. Alongside shoring up your company and strengthening its market position, you need to be able to get yourself in a position to help others adapt to the changing climate. Seeing opportunities requires an open mind.

To look for climate opportunities, do the exact same exercise you did to identify risks in the previous chapter: survey your company's physical environment, regulatory environment, and customer expectations, and look for potential changes. The only difference here is that this time, you'll look at those changes through the prism of opportunity. What can you do to contribute to mitigating climate change? How can you help people adapt?

# Where to Look for Opportunities

Climate change can trigger potentially monumental changes in both the physical environments—and the regulatory regimes. Both types of shifts can offer various opportunities for your company. These opportunities may include adopting low-emission energy sources, developing new products and services, entering new markets, and much more. CDP[1] directs companies to focus on five key areas to investigate for potential climate-related opportunities. To keep things consistent with this widely accepted framework, I will use the same categories of opportunities. But, as you will see, there is much space for interpretation, and creativity is certainly required to see all the ways in which your company can benefit from the seismic shifts ahead.

## *Resource Efficiency*

From a general perspective, resource efficiency refers to using resources wisely, minimizing waste, and getting the most value out of what we use. The ultimate goal here lies beyond simply "using less" but is to "decouple economic development from environmental degradation while ensuring that the transition to green economies creates opportunities and promotes well-being for all."[2] As with many other sustainability themes, resource efficiency is not a destination but a journey: Companies that pursue resource efficiency can gain a competitive edge by reducing costs and appealing to environmentally conscious consumers.

Research by McKinsey & Company indicates that resource efficiency can impact operating profits by up to 60 percent, and across different sectors, there's a notable correlation between companies' resource efficiency and their financial performance.[3] A separate study utilizing data from CDP's global climate database suggests that companies achieve an average internal rate of return ranging from 27 to 80 percent on their low-carbon investments.[4]

The measures your company takes to mitigate and adapt to climate change, such as recycling programs and energy-efficient equipment upgrades, can be no-brainer business opportunities in and of themselves. These programs have proven useful in reducing carbon footprints and trimming energy costs across sectors. For example, switching to LED light bulbs, if perhaps the lowest-hanging fruit of energy efficiency projects. We already discussed its benefits—LED lights last longer and use less energy than old incandescent ones. Don't forget recycling: papers, plastics, metals—every bit counts toward reducing our need for new materials and energy required to produce them. Carpooling or hopping on public transport instead of driving solo can also make a difference.

Many companies have long prioritized efficiency in production and distribution processes. Some of such measures have proven to be lucrative investments. The Dow Chemical Company, for example, invested nearly U.S. $2 billion between 1994 and 2010 to enhance resource efficiency, resulting in savings of U.S. $9.8 billion from reduced energy and wastewater consumption during manufacturing.[5] General electric slashed its greenhouse gas emissions by 32 percent and water use by 45 percent compared to baseline levels set in 2004 and 2006, respectively, yielding savings of U.S. $300 million.[6] Aeon Group, a Japanese retail giant, achieved a 9.7 percent reduction in food waste between 2015 and 2018, translating to ¥1 million in net sales.[7] Nike implemented modern cutting equipment in its factories, reducing footwear manufacturing waste and saving U.S. $12 million while repurposing nearly 1.2 million kilograms of material in 2018.[8] Walmart improved the fuel efficiency of its fleet by 87 percent over a decade through better routing, cargo loading, and driver training, resulting in savings of nearly U.S. $11 million and the avoidance of 15,000 metric tons of $CO_2$ emissions in 2014 alone.[9] A consumer goods giant, Unilever, has developed a comprehensive Climate Transition Action Plan covering its entire value chain and including actions such as improving logistics, reducing waste, optimizing packaging, increasing the use of renewable energy, and reducing emissions from refrigeration.[10]

Transportation is another sector where resource efficiency can go a long way in saving money—and reducing your company's carbon footprint. Improving automotive fuel efficiency is only the beginning. For example, Maersk, a leading global shipping company, has been systematically investing in energy-efficient ships.[11] Every electric truck or bus you see on the road is an element of the same low-carbon future to which we all aspire. By the way, the UK's electric double-decker bus sales tripled in 2023 compared with 2022, increasing the share of zero-emission models on the roads.[12] Meanwhile, micromobility companies provide a low-carbon alternative to private cars—and help companies just like yours reduce their carbon footprints.

The practice of recycling has a long history, with the majority of U.S. households having access to residential recycling services for paper, plastic, and glass bottles and jars. But the commercial sector, where waste is rampant and opportunities for recycling are limited, opens up a significant opportunity for improvement. While the entire circular ecosystem is still in the early stages of development, there are signs of progress, such as opportunities to reduce packaging or recycle certain unwanted items to give them a new life. Large companies such as Coca-Cola are addressing this issue through high-profile company-wide initiatives like "World Without Waste," focusing on bottle-to-bottle recycling and developing packaging solutions to reduce plastic waste.[13] Yet many others are also taking steps such as reducing packaging and reusing materials to promote circularity. Smaller companies are constantly coming to the market to provide collection and recycling solutions for used electronics, clothing, shoes, toys, and other hard-to-recycle items. And of course, there are startups, such as, for example, Cruz Foam,[14] looking for new ways to transform waste into valuable products. By repurposing shrimp and lobster aquaculture shells into an alternative to polystyrene styrofoam, Cruz Foam offers a commercially viable solution at a slight premium and with the potential for even lower costs in the future.

Resource efficiency plays out in the move toward more efficient buildings, which presents another set of business opportunities prompted by climate change. The U.S. Green Building Council, with its Leadership in Energy and Environmental Design certification, is the longest-standing leader in this space. As a more holistic alternative, the Green Building Institute offers its own certification for green buildings with a track specifically tailored for net-zero built assets. Opportunities in green construction abound. Real estate developers and construction companies are prioritizing energy efficiency and churning up buildings with minimal carbon footprints.

Companies of all sizes are engaging in renewable energy programs to reduce their carbon footprints. Switching to low-emission energy sources can also bring substantial long-term savings. For energy companies, replacing existing power plants with renewable energy can reduce costs system-wide, primarily by eliminating the cost of fossil fuel.[15] Commercial property owners can reduce their electricity bills by 75 percent by installing solar panels.[16] This is why owners of large commercial real estate—from big-box retailers to logistics and distribution center operators—are investing in on-site solar installations across their facilities, reducing reliance on electricity from the grid and slashing energy costs. Finally, multiple companies build their business on helping others improve resource efficiency—from Johnson Controls developing energy-efficient building solutions to parametric insurance* startups helping insurance underwriters save time and money processing claims.

## Use of Lower-Emission Energy Sources

Achieving climate goals is impossible without an energy transition toward low-carbon sources. The required shift away from fossil fuel-based energy sources, such as coal, oil, and natural gas, will take a global, concerted move toward cleaner energy alternatives. This requires both political will—and significant financial investment, estimated at approximately $7 trillion a year.[17] While already underway, the energy transition is expected to span decades. According to BloombergNEF, a significant portion of the projected $11.5 trillion investment in new

---

*Parametric insurance is a type of policy with pre-determined payouts tied to specific weather events rather than processed claims. It provides a new level of protection for smaller players in resource-dependent industries affected by climate change.

power generation capacity between 2018 and 2050 will be allocated to wind and solar energy technologies, along with other zero-carbon options, such as hydropower and nuclear power. Energy storage technologies and grid infrastructure required for integrating distributed renewable energy sources are also crucial components of this transition.

In addition to industry giants, small- and medium-sized companies are contributing to renewable energy solutions. These include offshore wind companies, such as Ørsted, located in Denmark, developing and operating large-scale wind farms to generate clean electricity. NextEra Energy, based in the United States, is one of the world's largest operators of wind and solar farms, providing low-carbon electricity to millions of customers. Geothermal solutions are gaining popularity, along with emerging technologies such as wave, tidal, and ocean current energy or concentrated solar power. There is a plethora of options—and a wide open space for inventors and entrepreneurs to innovate.

### Decarbonization Technologies

Decarbonizing our current economic system requires new technologies. The early 2020s have seen a boom in research into renewable energy, carbon sequestration technology, and low-carbon transportation solutions, often financed by government-backed green bonds. Investment firms, electronics makers, appliance companies, transportation companies, energy companies, and so on, all have a lucrative opportunity to invest in these technologies, receive government funding, and potentially realize massive returns.

Carbon removal and sequestration technologies represent an emerging frontier in environmental innovation, with the potential for substantial financial gains if successful. Direct air capture technologies [18] are now capable of extracting carbon dioxide directly from the atmosphere, while several companies are exploring methods to capture and reuse $CO_2$ at the source of emission. Both approaches hold promise for mitigating greenhouse gas emissions at scale.

Other opportunities related to decarbonization include a growing trend toward decentralized energy generation, from companies providing residential and commercial solar panel installations to manufacturers of solid oxide fuel cells that generate electricity on-site at homes and businesses. These cells offer a clean and reliable alternative to conventional power grids. Tesla's Powerwall home battery system[19] enables homeowners to store solar energy generated during the day for nighttime use, reducing dependence on the traditional grid and promoting energy independence.

## Products and Services

Climate change creates a demand for solutions. This opens up unique opportunities for your company to make investments in developing new products or services that can boost your revenue—in both short- and long term. Enter Joseph Wolf with Airlock Insulation,[20] a small but rapidly expanding company serving Ohio. Airlock Insulation helps its customers cut their energy savings by two-thirds by installing blown cellulose insulation. In addition to dramatically reducing heating and cooling costs, this type of insulation, consisting of 86 percent recycled fibers, is mold-resistant, provides excellent sound mitigation, and is nontoxic. Unlike fiberglass, it maintains its effectiveness in extreme temperatures.

Agtech and sustainable agriculture are gaining momentum in response to environmental concerns and changing consumer preferences. Beef and dairy farming, significant contributors to greenhouse gas emissions, are facing increasing demand for alternatives such as plant-based proteins (think Impossible Burger), lab-grown meat (such as UPSIDE Foods), and alternative proteins (such as Exo's cricket protein). Barclay's predicts the alternative meat market could reach $140 billion by 2029.[21] Biotech crops that are heat-tolerant and drought-resistant, along with climate-adaptive Agtech innovations, are also emerging as significant trends. In parallel, with climate-related changes affecting agricultural land availability, fertilizer producers are creating products that could improve yields while reducing their carbon footprint. Such high-performance fertilizers present opportunities for revenue growth in markets with strong demand for low-carbon products. On the flip side, there are microbial biofertilizers which can improve soil health and crop yields and potentially reduce reliance on synthetic fertilizers. And to top it off, there are seeds engineered to thrive in harsh conditions, helping farmers adapt to shifting weather patterns.

The future of transportation is electric, and the shift toward electrification extends beyond passenger cars to include buses, light-duty trucks, semis, ships, and even airplanes. Companies involved in developing electric vehicles (EVs), batteries, charging infrastructure, software, and alternative fuels technologies are poised to capitalize on market opportunities. Tesla leads the way in pioneering EVs, offering vehicles that substantially reduce greenhouse gas emissions compared with traditional gasoline-powered cars. And to help expand inadequate charging networks, British supermarket Sainsbury's has launched a new EV charging business with the planned installation of 750 ultrarapid chargers powered by renewable energy in over 100 parking lots by the end of 2024.[22]

In another example, Ridepanda is a startup focused on addressing climate issues, helping companies rethink their approaches to benefits, and reducing their carbon footprint. In 2020, they transitioned from a direct-to-consumer model to serving corporate clients. Their ideal clients include technology companies, organizations with sustainability goals, city governments, law firms, and hospitals. Ridepanda takes a broad approach, seeing potential interest across various sectors, but emphasizes the importance of focusing on ROI[†] and building a strong business case.

Ridepanda's innovative business model reflects a shift toward longer-term relationships with vehicles, moving away from short-term rentals toward ownership. They recognize the diversity of form factors and usage scenarios, offering a marketplace where customers can find the right vehicle based on their preferences and needs. Initially starting with an online retailer called Ridefinder, they aimed to provide personalized recommendations for vehicles tailored to individual requirements. This innovative approach demonstrates Ridepanda's commitment to sustainability and customer-centric solutions in the transportation sector.

---

[†]ROI (Return on Investment) is a performance indicator used to assess the profitability of an investment by comparing its net profit to its initial cost.

We have reached a critical juncture at which climate adaptation is paramount for planetary—and societal—well-being. This is why there is a growing focus on adaptation solutions—including financial solutions. For example, Ulrich Seitz, a veteran of the German renewables industry, is creating a venture capital (VC) network to invest in adaptation projects. Service providers which support disaster response efforts see demand for their services grow. We are talking everything from postdisaster debris removal and recycling following extreme weather events to comprehensive emergency response services, including emergency shelter management and environmental remediation. Analytics platforms and insurance risk solutions are also in high demand. There are parametric insurance products specifically crafted to address climate-related risks, such as floods, droughts, and wildfires, assisting businesses and individuals with managing the financial impacts of climate change. Engineering firms like AECOM now provide services like flood risk assessments, coastal protection design, and climate-resilient infrastructure development.[23]

Multiple companies are developing climate-resilient products, crafting building materials—such as flood-resistant coatings or heat-resistant roofing—tough enough to withstand extreme weather. Water filtration and purification systems are being developed to bolster climate resilience, particularly in regions vulnerable to water scarcity exacerbated by climate change.

Climate adaptation cannot work without common and sometimes even low-tech products. Climate control products like refrigerated cargo become essential as temperatures rise. Heat-resistant building materials, such as reflective roofing and special paints, are needed to withstand extreme heat. With wildfires and dust storms becoming more frequent, concerns about air quality become vital. This boosts the demand for air purifiers and filtration systems for homes and businesses. Finally, clothing designed for hotter climates can gain traction in certain areas. These examples highlight just a slice of the climate adaptation pie; specific needs will vary based on location and the nature of climate change impacts.

Consumer preferences are undergoing a significant shift, driven by environmental concerns and an increasing focus on the climate crisis, supported in the United States by both environmental awareness and well-timed government incentives. EVs, organic and plant-based food options, and "slow" fashion are all currently in style. In the financial sector, banks offer "green" mortgages with lower interest rates for energy-efficient homes, financing sustainable businesses and projects, which appeal to environmentally conscious customers who prioritize ethical investing.[24]

Last but not least, climate consulting space is flourishing, with a diverse set of players capitalizing on emerging opportunities. Startups, such as Jupiter and Persefoni, are leveraging climate data analytics and reporting to provide innovative solutions. Established consultancies, such as BCG and Bain, are expanding their services to include climate change strategy consulting. More specialized companies, such as ICF and Cadmus, focus on emissions measurement, modeling, and reporting services, offering essential support to organizations striving to understand and mitigate their environmental impacts.

### Changing Markets

As with any major shift, you will have a choice in defining your company's position toward climate-related market changes. Do you become the "first mover" and blaze new trails in search of elusive advantage? Or do you zero in on becoming a "fast follower," one that often reaps the benefits of more established—and less risky—markets? Do you see your company as a leader or a laggard? You do not have to do anything in particular, but companies which help mitigate climate change impacts, adapt to them, or cater to the changing needs and preferences of a climate-conscious world are positioned to create new markets and find success.

Climate change in and of itself is driving several shifts in customer demand. For example, a new need for artificial snow at ski resorts in the Alps has led the Israeli firm IDE to develop the first-of-its-kind All Weather Snowmaker device.[25] The EV market has exploded in response to climate anxiety, as has the personal solar panel market. And, given the increased demand for green energy, prices for the lithium and copper used in batteries have increased significantly. Additionally, the shifting trade routes have a consequential impact on the demand for location-specific trade infrastructure.

As global warming alters areas with permafrost,[†] it may unveil new arable land and a potential boon for agriculture. With the world's population expected to hit 8.6 billion by 2030 and 9.7 billion by 2050, the demand for food will steadily rise. In some countries, this growth will likely heighten reliance on their productive agricultural sector, driving increased demand for fertilizers. In the long run, fertilizer producers stand to gain from climate change impacts, population expansion, and shifting investor attitudes toward agriculture.

Chasing new market opportunities has established financial institutions venture into energy financing, recognizing the escalating demand for clean energy solutions. Some banks offer green financing in burgeoning developing markets, such as Africa, Latin America, China, or India, supporting clean energy ventures and leveraging the surge in the demand for sustainable infrastructure. Others provide financial services for EV technology companies and charging infrastructure development, aligning with the rapid expansion of the EV industry.

To direct investment toward technologies and infrastructure required for climate mitigation and adaptation, many governments support climate initiatives by offering a range of incentives to companies of all sizes. First, there are tax credits for those who invest in renewable energy, such as solar panels or wind turbines. These credits can take the sting out of the upfront costs and make low-carbon energy options more appealing. All EV producers are reaping the rewards of government tax credits and incentives aimed at boosting EV production and deployment, effectively slashing the price tag on EVs for consumers. The incentive game isn't just limited to big players; even smaller EV dealerships are cashing in while making EVs more wallet-friendly and enticing for buyers. Up-and-comers, such as Kia and Hyundai, are

---

[†]Permafrost is permanently frozen ground that remains below 0°C for at least two consecutive years.

challenging Tesla's leadership position in the U.S. market and shaking up the entire EV landscape.

Meanwhile, companies in other sectors are also tapping into government incentives. Offshore wind projects receive subsidies and feed-in tariffs from governments in Europe and Asia, encouraging investment in renewable energy infrastructure. Power companies use tax credits and renewable energy certificates to support their investments in solar and wind energy projects in developing countries. Smaller companies are leveraging federal and state-level tax credits to offer homeowners savings on things like solar panel installations or installing energy-efficient HVAC systems in commercial buildings, helping businesses cut energy costs.

There are other incentives for companies that are interested in entering emerging markets for climate-related products and services. Such incentives include grants and low-interest loans for businesses interested in things like upgrading to energy-efficient lighting or beefing up insulation. Your company could be an urban farm—or you could be installing green roofs or renting bikes to tourists. There are grants for setting up textile recycling facilities—and for scaling used clothes collection efforts. There are loans for collecting discarded food from restaurants and grocery stores, diverting it from landfills, and turning it into compost. Selling and distributing recycled building materials could also qualify. If you need additional motivation, look at BlackRock. This investment giant is leveraging government tax credits and subsidies to beef up their investment portfolios with renewable energy projects.

As carbon pricing initiatives emerge, companies can participate in carbon offset marketplaces by implementing projects that reduce emissions or remove carbon dioxide from the atmosphere. Existing cap-and-trade programs typically focus on large emitters, such as power plants, industrial facilities, or heavy manufacturers, which limit revenue opportunities for smaller companies. As regulatory regimes mature and potentially allocate reduction targets to a wider range of companies, they can generate revenue and contribute to climate action.

There's a bustling industry of service providers aiding companies in navigating their journey toward climate readiness. Among them are data analytics firms crafting risk assessment tools and models to assist businesses and communities in bracing for climate-related disruptions. Carbon offset project developers are working with entities seeking to mitigate their environmental impact by engaging in carbon markets. Brokers are assisting companies in purchasing carbon offsets to meet emissions trading regulations. Consultants of various specialties, accountants, technology providers, and myriad others contribute to this landscape, offering tailored solutions to meet the unique needs of each entity striving to adapt to the challenges posed by climate change. In the words of Michael Poisson, the CEO of Ideal Ratings and a veteran of the ESG rankings space: "There is unlimited opportunity for small-, medium-, and large-sized service providers to offer reporting, consulting, audit, and assurance services to every member of the ESG life cycle—framework provider, reporting entity, investment company, investor, regulator, and so on."[26]

## Resilience

Climate resilience is tightly linked to climate adaptation, a topic of great contention and perhaps even greater importance. Both mitigation and adaptation measures are necessary in addressing climate change. While mitigation has traditionally garnered more attention from public and private sector decision makers than adaptation, there is a growing realization that taking concerted action on climate adaptation deserves at least equal recognition. Given the inertia of the Earth's climate system and the life-changing nature of readily unavoidable impacts of climate change, adaptation is an urgent imperative for the peace and well-being of current and future generations.

Climate adaptation opportunities focus on what individual companies can do to adjust to the impacts of climate change. These actions tend to be industry-specific and dependent on local context. For example, companies can explore resource substitutes and diversification strategies to mitigate risks associated with climate change and resource scarcity, particularly caused by supply chain disruptions. IKEA sourcing recycled wood and bamboo, a rapidly renewable resource, is an example of an action that has both mitigation and adaptation impacts.

Companies sourcing agricultural inputs are also closely examining the resilience of their suppliers in the face of various climate scenarios. Up along the value chain, agricultural producers are investing in drought-resistant crops, regenerative farming practices, and improved water management techniques to ensure long-term food security. Their customers, such as McDonald's and Nestlé, are proactively addressing the risks associated with agricultural supply chains. Other players are capitalizing on emerging opportunities in this evolving market, including carbon sequestration through "regenerative agriculture."

In the financial services sector, resilience-focused products and services involve offering specialized insurance products for climate-related events. A parametric flood insurance product tailored for small businesses is a good example of such a product. Enhancing climate resilience of the investment chain involves strategies, such as ESG integration, stress testing, and robust risk management, all of which require advanced data and analytics. Thankfully, there are service providers that harness weather data and artificial intelligence to offer real-time weather risk assessments to businesses and investors.

In real estate, flood protection and climate-resilient infrastructure are top priorities.[27] Real Estate Investment Trusts (REITs) and property companies are factoring climate impacts into site selection, fortifying at-risk buildings against flooding, and installing renewable energy systems for emergency power. Manufacturing companies are developing processes and technologies that are less vulnerable to climate disruptions, such as flooding or power outages. The financial services industry is here to help as well with resilient infrastructure investment trusts,[28] which prioritize projects designed to withstand extreme weather events.

### What Else?

As you see, there are myriad climate-related opportunities, ranging from obvious to outlandish. A separate book could be written just to describe all the ways in which companies can make money while helping others mitigate or adapt to the impacts of climate change. But creating an encyclopedia of potential climate-related opportunities was not my goal. The pace of change in the business world as we know it all but guarantees that the moment this book landed in your lap—or on your Kindle—such a list would be hopelessly obsolete.

I hope, however, that learning about these solutions has wet your appetite and got your creative juices flowing. These emerging solutions—what is—constitute a miniscule portion of what could be. To bring some structure to this "opportunity blind spot," I suggest organizing your thinking along the following lines. Imagine that you wake up on a beautiful morning. The year is 2050. Over the past quarter century, you have been running a successful company. What is it that your company produces? Who needs it and why? What chain of events brought about this specific set of environmental, market, and regulatory conditions?

While quantifying the profits of your company in the year 2050 may be ... well ... challenging, the long-term trend is clear: Climate readiness is not just "good PR," it's good business. So, take stock of the full range of the climate-related opportunities described earlier in this chapter and imagine how you might integrate similar ideas into your organizational strategy. Then ask the magic question: "What else?" As you begin answering this question, keep going. Don't stop.

The last—and most important—step in this exercise is to assume that the future you have just described is much closer than you think. It is not a "someday, maybe" kind of future. Do not underestimate how climate readiness can transform your company. My experience working on both the startup and investment management sides of the entrepreneurial ecosystem, as well as a research arm of an international financial institution, has convinced me that if you are able to fathom it, that means right now, as we speak, there are people working tirelessly to create those breakthrough products or services, figure out profitable business models, shape the regulatory landscape, and even finance them.

And so can you.

## The Cost of Missed Opportunity

According to a 2019 survey conducted by the nonprofit CDP, a whopping 225 out of the world's 500 largest companies revealed that they saw climate-related opportunities as potential financial gains totaling over $2.1 trillion.[29] That's not chump change; it's a colossal sum that illustrates the immense potential for businesses to capitalize on climate-friendly initiatives. For companies, climate opportunities can bring several financial benefits such as cutting operating costs, earning more from products and services suddenly in demand, accessing new markets, or expanding production capacity. Businesses may also find it easier to get funding and see their assets increase in value. In finance, there's potential for portfolios to grow as assets rise in value, especially with investments in low-emission technology.

Despite the grandiosity of potential opportunities, pinpointing exactly what individual companies miss out by doing nothing about climate change is difficult. The markets are still evolving, and many climate-related impacts haven't fully materialized. Forget "normal" markets—they don't exist anymore. The opportunities arising from climate change are inherently industry- and location-specific. For example, financial services firms can help investors snap up land that will increase in value as the climate changes. Likewise, agricultural companies can buy land in cold-weather areas for cheap, and it will become desirable as temperatures rise.

Some climate opportunities are a clear no-brainer. For example, upgrading to LED lighting can save a company 50 to 80 percent on lighting costs,[30] with payback periods often within one to two years. This is what Oliver Winter at a&o Hostels experienced firsthand, just like many other companies. But climate opportunities extend well beyond cost reductions. Sustainability in general—and climate readiness in particular—is the new engine for innovation and growth, and companies which ignore it risk getting left behind. Remember Blockbuster scoffing at Netflix?[31] That kind of missed opportunity can cost millions or even your entire company. One thing is true: Entire industries are getting uprooted these days. This means insights from seemingly unrelated fields can be gold. And we can already tell that some companies have missed the boat on significant climate-driven trends.

The coal industry serves as a stark example of failing to adapt to changing times. Many coal companies stubbornly clung to their outdated practices, failing to embrace renewables as demand for cleaner energy surged. The consequence? Massive stock price plunges and a string of bankruptcies. Peabody Energy, a major player in coal production, even had to file for bankruptcy not once but twice.[32]

And it's not just coal. Big Oil is also dragging its feet in the renewable race. Oil and gas companies have been slow to diversify their portfolios, leaving themselves vulnerable as governments worldwide pour resources into clean energy initiatives. Exxon, for instance, had to swallow a $20 billion writedown on its fossil fuel assets in 2020, a clear acknowledgment of the dwindling value of these holdings.[33] With the future of energy veering toward renewables, oil and gas companies risk being left in the dust, missing out on a multitrillion dollar market.

Legacy automakers have a tough choice to make as Tesla continues to dominate the EV market, and new entrants, such as Kia and Hyundai, emboldened by new federal incentives, aggressively pursue environmentally minded—or simply technology-curious—consumers. So far, traditional automakers have been slow to shift gears toward EVs in the U.S. market. The consequence? Risking not only losing market share but also potentially missing out on billions in future EV sales.

With the spotlight shining bright on waste reduction, companies in the waste management sector need to step up their game. Those stuck in the old-school mentality of getting paid to collect trash could find themselves left in the dust as companies divert more and more of their waste from landfill. The real winners in this space are those pioneering recycling and circular economy solutions. By finding ways to reuse and minimize waste, these innovators are opening up new streams of revenue. Similar dynamics affect construction companies who may be slow to adopt green building practices. Just take a look at the numbers: The global green building market is expected to reach $1.3 trillion by 2030.[34] That's a huge opportunity for those who seize it, and a big missed chance for those who don't.

The growth potential for climate-friendly products and services is significant across various sectors. For example, the global sustainable packaging market is forecasted to reach $469 billion by 2027.[35] The market for renewable energy is also booming, with estimates suggesting that it will reach $1.5 trillion by 2025.[36] These are just a few examples. The key takeaway is that companies that fail to adapt to changing market conditions risk missing out on significant business opportunities. The vast majority of large—and many small and midsize companies— have already been making strides toward climate readiness. Yet without a shift in perspective and the willingness to recognize and seize opportunities amidst the social, economic, and political upheavals that accompany climate change, corporate climate action will likely stay a cost center at best—and a box-checking exercise at worst.

Despite our best efforts, climate change is here to stay. Ultimately, the scale and momentum of climate mitigation and adaptation efforts will depend on private actors and their ability to see and act on new opportunities. There is much that can—and should—be done to counteract the effects of the exploitative and wasteful approach much of humanity has been applying toward the environment—and itself. This means replacing the thoughtless consumerism that lies at the core of the climate crisis with a more holistic, long-term perspective—and a more urgent call for business leaders to step up to the plate in taking action. Your appetite for profits and impact can benefit us all.

# CHAPTER 6

# Keep Yourself Accountable

In 2019, thousands of employees of Microsoft, Amazon, Twitter, Google, Facebook, and Square walked out to protest their employers' lack of climate action. Days earlier, in an attempt to prevent the walkout, the tech giants threw together new initiatives involving electric vehicles and renewable energy. The rushed, cobbled-together nature of the companies' climate plans and responses made them look opportunistic at best and deceptive at worst. Instead of canceling the walkout, the organizers redoubled their efforts and made sweeping, specific demands for the companies to drop their contracts with oil and gas companies and to stop their donations to certain politicians.[1] Although this set of demands was not met, the strike became a catalyst for each of these companies to initiate impactful climate initiatives, as it set the stage for continuing media scrutiny of their ongoing engagements with the oil and gas industry[2] and demonstrated the power of such initiatives to usher change.

Stopping your employees from quitting is important, but this chapter is not just about keeping them happy. This is about building a company on a foundation of integrity, where what we say actually matches what we do. Let's face it: There's a lot of hot air out there with companies blowing their own horn on their sustainability efforts. Political considerations or simple convenience can cloud the sharpest business judgment. Businesses are notorious for talking a big game and then ... well ... not following through. But you can be different. It's a golden opportunity to build a foundation of integrity in your business. Let's face it: There's a lot of hot air out there, especially on climate issues. Businesses are notorious for overpromising and underdelivering or just plain greenwashing. Here's your chance to be a beacon of integrity. Because guess what? Integrity is the only way to get things done. You know that deep down. This chapter is your guide on how to back up your words with some real action.

## Internalizing Externalities

Why exactly would you want to walk the walk when it comes to climate readiness? You may have heard it all about customers being fed up with greenwashing, regulators coming up with increasingly onerous reporting requirements, or corporate social responsibility being simply a "must-have" for any self-respecting company looking to thrive in our day and age. All of these concerns are real, but addressing each of them would likely have you end up in the realm of "box-checking" on climate rather than explaining why it is in your best interest actually to do the right thing.

Enter "internalization of externalities," a foundational concept in environmental economics. Arthur Pigou, a British economist, introduced the concept in the 1920s.[3] The idea is that economic transactions can have costs or benefits affecting third parties and, thus, fall outside the market system. Think of them as value—or losses—not paid for by the party receiving the benefit. Seems unfair, right? To solve the issue, Pigou floated the idea of taxes designed to make the polluter or the party causing negative externalities bear the full cost of the harm they cause. This would make them essentially "internalize" those external costs.

Climate-related externalities are many: From damage to public infrastructure to public health impacts to ecosystem loss, they are by default not factored into the polluters' costs. The ultimate goal here is to impact business decisions: By putting a price on greenhouse gas (GHG) emissions, we create a financial incentive to reduce emissions and pollute less. At least the European Environment Agency sees internalization of externalities this way, that is, as "incorporation of an externality into the market decision-making process through pricing or regulatory interventions."[4]

Implementing mechanisms to charge companies for their GHG emissions can significantly alter the choices made by both businesses and consumers. Imagine companies forking over just one dollar per ton of their GHG emissions. One dollar is not much, but this extra cost would add up and push companies to find ways to emit less. They might revamp their waste management setup, invest in renewable energy, or simply look for ways to be more energy-efficient.

But it's not just the businesses that would feel the pinch. A carbon fee would increase production costs, and, in turn, the prices of goods and services that rely on fossil fuels could go up as well. This could make consumers think twice before grabbing conventional, carbon-intensive products. They might opt for things with lower carbon footprints or cut down on consumption altogether. Putting a price on GHG emissions shakes up the game for everyone involved, making us all rethink our choices.

By 2023, approximately 23 percent of global emissions fell under carbon pricing initiatives, and as of 2024, almost 40 countries and over 30 subnational regions are implementing these measures. Some regions have set prices exceeding $25 per ton.[5] France, for instance, introduced an eco-tax of €1.50 on domestic and intra-European flights and €3 on flights outside the European Union (EU) in 2018. Additionally, starting in 2020, business class seats on EU flights incur a €9 eco-charge, while longer flights tack on €18. The French government anticipates raising €180 million annually from these flight taxes, earmarked for alternative transportation like trains. For Air France, this tax is expected to add €60 million yearly to expenses. At this level, the price signal could be strong enough to prompt the airline to buy more efficient planes.[6]

In essence, carbon pricing systems nudge businesses and consumers toward climate-friendly choices. They foster accountability by holding polluters responsible for the environmental and social costs of their activities. All regulations are heading in this direction. Established markets such as the EU offer a roadmap for how regulatory advancements might unfold. If you keep an eye on regulatory changes in the United States and other places, you'll notice that almost all of them revolve around internalizing externalities. Maintaining your social license to operate means that sooner or later, your company will be held accountable for its climate impact. From a capitalist standpoint, it's simply about fairness.

## Plan Your Work

By now, you already get that implementing a climate strategy should steer your company toward a sustainable path marked by cutting GHG emissions. Reducing your carbon footprint is half of the equation—the other half is to make sure your products stay competitive in the market, your company stays profitable, and your investors stay happy. And this is quite a journey. This is why you need a solid plan of action to bring it all together. We have discussed such plans in the previous chapters. But to make it all work, your plan should also lay out a roadmap with rules, organization tweaks, and tech upgrades to cut emissions and keep things moving in the right direction.

Your company's financial health, from investment levels to profitability and beyond, hinges on your adeptness at seamlessly integrating climate risks and opportunities across various aspects of your operations. This includes embedding them into your business strategy, protocols for monitoring and managing risks, investment strategies, and financial planning processes. It also involves effectively collecting and managing climate-related data, ensuring accurate information, consistent monitoring, methodology updates, and verification. Bridging the gap between targets and implementation requires both execution and strategic capabilities, with a cautious approach to setting priorities and defining the core DNA of your product or company. It's crucial not to hastily shift priorities but instead chart well-defined journeys toward sustainability.

### Climate Strategy and Decarbonization Plan

A climate strategy is your company's roadmap for addressing climate change. It should address both climate change mitigation and adaptation. In other words, you need to think through reducing your company's carbon footprint—and also the actions you need to take to adapt to the shifting climatic and regulatory conditions. Your climate strategy should lay out a clear vision statement to articulate the company's commitment to climate readiness and its role in combating climate change. Clarity around key priorities sets the tone and gets everyone on board, from employees to stakeholders. Your climate strategy should be based on an honest assessment of your company's carbon footprint and climate-related risks. Focus on identifying opportunities for innovation, cost savings, and market leadership in the transition to a low-carbon economy while adapting to climate change impacts.

In addition climate strategies, some companies develop decarbonization plans as a roadmap to slash their GHG emissions. These plans typically focus on reducing emissions within their own operations and throughout their supply chain, emphasizing energy and fuel efficiency, transportation improvements, and logistics optimization—all of the areas we addressed in Chapter 2. A decarbonization plan is like a playbook—it's practical, detailed, and action-oriented. It should take climate strategy and break it down into clear steps and actions to take to cut GHG emissions. The plan should hone in on measurable reductions in carbon emissions, laying out targets, timelines, and strategies to hit those marks. And it's not just about setting goals; it's about tracking them, too, with clear metrics to measure progress along the way.

To develop your decarbonization plan, start with baseline emissions across all three scopes: direct emissions from your facilities (Scope 1), indirect emissions from purchased energy (Scope 2), and other indirect emissions from your value chain (Scope 3). Identify key emission sources to prioritize reduction efforts. Next, set goals and targets for GHG emission reduction, preferably aligning with net-zero objectives and ideally based on scientific evidence as per the Paris Agreement. Develop specific strategies to reduce carbon emissions from those sources which contribute the most to your carbon footprint—and which you can realistically address. Make plans for offsetting the rest of your emissions if necessary.

Depending on your industry and the size of your company, this work may involve drafting project documentation to upgrade and enhance the energy efficiency of your production lines, developing feasibility studies for technology investments, evaluating market potential for climate-friendly products, revising your capital improvement plans to align the timing of major equipment purchases with your energy efficiency upgrades, reassessing your sourcing practices, and renegotiating contracts to switch raw materials and fuels. Obviously, you might be working with engineers, accountants, sustainability special- ists, sourcing managers, and other professionals across your company. The outcome of your decarbonization efforts will be a business model characterized by minimal GHG emissions.

A single document could include your climate strategy and decarbonization plan. For a small company, it can start as a list of simple bullet points. For larger companies, it may involve consultations with stakeholders, multiple departments, or contracting with outside consultants for engineering or management support. Keep in mind that climate strategies are often more flexible and can evolve over time as new technologies, regulations, and societal expectations emerge.

The biggest—and often fatal—mistake in developing climate strategies is to have no connection to the company's business strategy. This disconnect shows up in different ways. As a result, some companies are left with escalating expenses and time spent on reporting on what seems like an ever-expanding set of disjointed metrics, activities, and initiatives. Others start with tactics and just focus on specific initia- tives that "feel right" or "sound good." After putting much thought, effort, and resources into climate programs, companies find themselves struggling to understand how this activity can support their financial bottom line. As societal expectations for businesses evolve, leaders increasingly expect sustainability initiatives to deliver tangible business benefits. Unfortunately, many programs lack the foundation needed to achieve this alignment right from the start.

The integration I am talking about is not a destination; it's a conscious, well-paced journey. As your company works to define its approach to climate change and develop an appropriate response, many conversations will need to take place at different levels to get things going. You might find yourself serving as both an instigator and educator, guiding and coaching others through this journey.

## Policies, Processes, and Procedures

The decarbonization plan is only the tip of the iceberg—multiple systems, processes, and procedures are required to enable it. As you put those things in place, you will lay the foundation for continuing business success well beyond a one-time effort. At a minimum, I recommend addressing several areas.

First, while climate considerations may not always be explicit, they should be incorporated into your company's overall strategy. This means updating your company's strategic plan to reflect a climate strategy and a decarbonization plan. Several components are likely to be affected. Your vision and mission statement may now include a nod to sustainability and—if appropriate—climate action, particularly if they are tightly linked to your company's other aspirations. Strategic goals, such as growth and profitability, may now include net-zero emissions by a certain date, as well as climate adaptation and resilience aspirations. Your competitor and market analysis should now include decarbonization trends or standards within your industry. What are your competitors doing? What role do you want to play in the low-carbon economy of the future? Are there any opportunities to lead the industry in turning climate action into sustainable and profitable business model innovation?

Second, streamline processes for tracking emissions data. Identify which department will lead regular climate reporting and figure out how they will interact with other departments to collect data and create reports. This may involve implementing new software or systems for collecting and analyzing data, as well as establishing clear protocols for documentation and reporting.

Then, amend key policies and procedures, including risk management, sourcing, investment guidelines, and other functional areas affected by your climate strategy and decarbonization plan. For instance, if capital deployment at your company undergoes scrutiny by the investment review committee, it may want to begin looking into how it may be linked to climate goals as part of their evaluation. What technologies and solutions can help accelerate your efforts? Educate your employees about these efforts and how they will affect their work. No one likes to be blindsided. You also want to implement this step in phases, beginning with the most impacted areas in the organization, to make sure that people have the time to absorb changes. And make sure to allocate the necessary financial resources for implementing your plans.

Think about—and map out business processes for—keeping a close eye on market conditions and jumping on climate-related opportunities. Establish a monitoring system and appropriate responses to climate-related regulations. If your organization has dedicated government relations and market research teams, they need to know what to look for. These professionals excel in connecting the dots, but it's on you to point out those climate-related dots for them in the first place. If your company is small, monitoring regulations and markets could fall on your shoulders. That's fine—just make sure you think through the new sources of information to keep an eye on and the steps to take to orchestrate organizational response when the time is right.

### Organization and Staffing

Organizational accountability begins with personal responsibility. This is why I recommend that, initially, you have someone in your organization be responsible for climate action. This person should be knowledgeable enough to understand not only the basics of climate footprint and climate risk management—but also the ins and outs of your company's strategic direction, operations, and culture. This person needs to be savvy enough to connect climate concerns with the realities of your business environment and your organizational context. Importantly, he or she should have the authority and diplomacy skills to engage with leaders across business units and functions inside your organization. This person could very well be you—especially after reading this book. But, if not, you know what to look for.

The "climate tzar" role should be temporary. Over time, he or she should be replaced by a team of organizational champions to tackle emissions and climate challenges—and to keep the momentum going. To ease the transition, identify key roles and skill sets needed to effectively address climate issues. At this stage, do not think about personalities—you want to focus on the skills you *need* for your efforts to succeed, not just the skills you *have* in your organization. Your "climate team" should include technical and engineering experts—but also colleagues with expertise in finance and environmental science. This team will conduct comprehensive assessments of current emissions and develop strategies to reduce them. This means that the team should be able to develop and evaluate project proposals from both technical and financial standpoints. This may also include assessing market trends, conducting cost-benefit analyses, and evaluating the feasibility of technologies and processes. The climate team will also evaluate the potential impacts of climate change on your company's operations and develop risk management and climate adaptation plans.

Depending on your company's needs and resources, you may be bringing in new talent and expertise. This will have you creating job descriptions, defining reporting structures, and identifying key performance indicators to measure progress. Be careful not to saddle your organization with a contingent of smooth-talking. Even more importantly, make sure to provide training and resources to help the people you already have to be effective in implementing climate strategies. Climate issues should be included in professional training, retraining, and advanced training programs for personnel at all levels. This involves integrating climate-related topics into existing training programs or developing new training modules focused on climate science, sustainability, and energy management.

Everyone, from the CEO down, must be held accountable for reaching climate goals. A small pack of rogue anticlimate Vice Presidents (VPs) can stall even a best-in-class strategy. But their perspective can still be valuable in pointing out the issues or inconsistencies in your strategies and identifying potential challenges. Welcome constructive criticism and invite healthy discussion.

The best way to ensure everyone is on board is to embed climate into the very DNA of your company. One effective tactic is to connect progress toward climate goals directly to compensation. Some of my clients, for example, have instituted bonuses for managers who find new emission-reducing processes or even have tied portions of salaries to achieving specific climate goals. Some business leaders might worry that such incentives will damage morale, but the opposite tends to be true. Employees appreciate such programs, and having them can help attract and retain top talent. In a 2018 survey conducted by Carbon Credentials of employees from a cross section of companies with 250-plus employees, 66 percent of UK employees supported bonuses tied to cutting carbon emissions. And yet, only 4 percent of the companies in the survey had such incentives in place.[7]

If you are still worried, consider using nonfinancial ways to reward employees who help you hit your climate goals. This might include bonuses, awards, employee spotlights, and green product discounts. In many cases, opportunities for personal and professional growth—or recognition of employee's contribution to the company and the community—can be more valuable than strictly financial incentives. Be creative!

## Data and Analytics

None of these strategizing, planning, process re-engineering, hiring, training, or incentivizing measures will happen without data. You will need a system to collect the information required to calculate your carbon footprint and assess your climate risks. This system can be a simple Excel spreadsheet, a full-scale integrated solution like Watershed, or anything in between. We discussed selecting a solution to handle your carbon footprint assessments in Chapter 2. In addition, you may consider solutions—or modules—to support climate risk management or life cycle assessments (LCAs).

Building the infrastructure to collect, monitor, and verify all these data can be expensive, but the investment will pay off. It will allow you to track progress, make sure people take the steps they commit to, tweak the climate plan when necessary, and easily report accomplishments to climate certification agencies, investors, regulators, employees, and company leaders. Don't be afraid to get your hands dirty and make sure to dig into specific accounting transactions to fully understand how things work at your company.

Leveraging AI offers the potential for precise and timely responses to climate risks. For example, the use of AI can help optimize resource usage in farming, from water to fertilizers, by analyzing historical crop yield data alongside current weather patterns to predict future yields. AI can enhance climate modeling and even devise adaptation strategies. It can be your friend in building resilient supply chains as well as in water resource management, energy optimization, and disaster response.

## Work Your Plan

In April of 2021, Jeff Bezos, the founder of Amazon, publicly advocated for an increase in the corporate tax rate. Shortly after, it came out that Amazon had paid an effective tax rate of 9.4 percent in 2020—in stark contrast to what he advocated. Politicians and talking heads promptly panned Bezos and Amazon as hypocrites. Bezos' posturing, genuine or not, did him much more PR harm than good.

To avoid a similar fate, make sure your public climate stance aligns with your strategy, values, and goals and that it contributes to your long-term profitability not just a short-term market positioning. This, of course, is in addition to telling the truth.

As you work on putting your climate strategy into action, keep your ego in check. It's not about trying to be trendy or signaling a political stance to impress others. Instead of just ticking the boxes of what's right, be vocal about your efforts and demonstrate to others that sustainability is achievable and practical. Strive to become a trailblazer in your industry by leading by example and showing what's possible.

### Focus on Results

The key to being an agent of change is to keep your focus on results. Already, most companies take great pleasure in reporting on their climate strategies, but they tend to report on what is easy to observe: their actions, investments, or engagement "encounters" with customers and other stakeholders. They rarely, if ever, report on their total environmental impact and the *outcomes* their actions generate.

Results are harder to measure, but they're what actually matter. A successful climate strategy sets and tracks key performance indicators that relate to their actual environmental impact. That way, instead of saying, "We have invested $15 million in decarbonization technology," you can say, "We have invested $15 million to implement low-carbon technology in all of our worksites, resulting in a 4-percent reduction in GHG emissions since last year." If you install LED lighting features, focus on the percentage reduction in energy consumption. You may be running enjoyable and engaging reuse and recycling programs, but what percentage of your products or materials is recovered and reintroduced into the production cycle? If you are paying for your employees using public transportation, what is the actual decrease in the carbon footprint of employees who commute to work? At the beginning of your climate readiness journey, you may not be able to answer questions like these. In fact, you may even be fuzzy on which questions you *should* be asking. It could be wise to seek consultant guidance—but don't over-rely on external experts. Keep your internal data yours and make sure you have full understanding of all the ins and outs of your climate impacts.

Conducting an LCA, as discussed in Chapter 3, will help you quantify the total $CO_2e$ emissions associated with your products or services from cradle to grave. To add more weight to your numbers, consider getting a third-party verification for your company's GHG emissions inventory. This outside review can add credibility to your climate reporting and ultimately build trust with stakeholders. When a respected organization puts a stamp of approval on your emissions data, this effectively tells investors, customers, and regulators that your numbers are solid and unbiased. The added transparency can make your company look good in the eyes of eco-conscious investors and customers. Depending on your industry, this reputational boost can easily translate into a competitive edge.

The verification process can pressure-test your reporting procedures. It will dig out any glitches or slip-ups in how you collect and report your data. This, of course, is not ideal, but at the very least, you will gain valuable insights. The verification report can also clue you in on areas where you could tweak your strategies for cutting emissions, helping you improve over time.

Getting third-party verification for your climate reporting starts with finding a qualified verifier. Look for accredited bodies with experience in your industry. Make sure they're independent of your company to ensure an unbiased assessment. Resources, such as the Climate Registry,[8] can help you find the right verifiers. During the verification process, the verifier will review your emissions data, methodology, and reporting processes. Be ready to discuss them in detail. The verifier might also talk to your team or inspect your site. Once it is done, you will get a verification report. The report will detail his or her findings and state whether your emissions report meets the reporting standard you chose. It might also include suggestions for improvement. Keep in mind, this is not an assessment of your company's carbon footprint, just the way you calculate it.

### Use Offsets Wisely

At some point, no matter how ambitious your decarbonization plans are or how much you excel at hitting your targets, you will hit a wall. After you have harvested the low-hanging fruit, some of the remaining actions will require too much effort to implement. You may have tasked your product team with designing carbon out of the entire value chain, and what's now left is there to stay. Or perhaps you have already rethought—and transformed—your entire business model. Maybe some decarbonization efforts need to be shelved for a while until the necessary technology is there—or until they make economic sense. And if you are in the net-zero game, it is by definition impossible to achieve success without offsetting some of the carbon emissions remaining after you have taken all the reduction actions you could.

Then—and only then—would I recommend investing in high-quality carbon offset projects to compensate for unavoidable emissions. There are many ways to buy carbon credits, each suited to different needs and preferences. For smaller companies or those with limited credit requirements, retailers like Terrapass and Nori offer accessible options, granting access to diverse projects and managing the retirement process. Alternatively, brokers act as intermediaries, assisting in finding credits tailored to specific criteria and handling transactions akin to other commodities. For those seeking more direct engagement, contracting with project developers is viable, particularly for large credit volumes, though it necessitates additional negotiation efforts and retirement management. Emerging online platforms also streamline carbon credit transactions, providing further convenience in the process.

When purchasing carbon credits, there are several things to watch out for. First, the good old "trust but verify" principle applies here. Just as with any emerging market space, there is ample potential for fraud. Prioritize transparency, opting for sellers who offer comprehensive details about the projects and the credits' impact. Look for endorsement by respected registries, such as Verra or Gold Standard, to ensure the credits meet rigorous environmental and social criteria.

Remember that credits are tied to specific emission reduction projects, so make sure that they align the chosen projects with your company's sustainability objectives. For example, projects could support renewable energy, energy efficiency, or forest preservation. Some of them will contribute more directly to your company's mission, which is an added bonus on top of buying your way out of public scrutiny.

### Maintain Narrative Alignment

There are many ways to communicate your position and actions in the sustainability space. But before you get to choose the best social media channels to broadcast your messaging to the world, make sure to focus on results. Most companies take great pleasure in reporting on their environmental or community initiatives, but they communicate only about what is easy to observe: their own actions or investments. They rarely, if ever, report on their total impact, and the results their actions generate. It is not a surprise, then, that there is a groundswell of public demand for transparency and integrity when it comes to sustainability. The public's—and regulators'—tolerance for greenwashing is rapidly diminishing. Granted, the outcomes of our actions can be difficult to measure, but they are much more powerful in painting a true picture of companies' intent and impact.

Make sure that your public position on climate issues aligns with your strategy, values, and goals and that it contributes to your long-term profitability not just a short-term market positioning. Then, work to keep everyone internally, especially senior leadership, aligned on the message in public. Consider appropriate "guardrails" for outside communication, such as guidelines for social media engagement on climate-related topics. Make sure your employees have effective channels to have their voices heard and prove your responsiveness to what your customers bring up.

Most importantly, take your communication about climate seriously. Government agencies, consumers, environmental watchdogs, investors, and armies of analysts are watching. According to Michael Poisson, the author of *ESG Revolution,* "advertising activities also became a target to observe ESG behavior."[9] The new AI and natural language processing capabilities make it easy to collect and analyze massive volumes of unstructured data to decipher insights about the actual environmental performance of your company. In some cases, they can "analyze the spoken words by a company's leadership during quarterly earnings calls, specifically ... positive or negative intonations in these words to assess the company's impact on environmental issues."[10] It pays to tell the truth—and to walk the walk on climate readiness.

Whether you like it or not, you are standing on a bigger stage now. Climate change has illustrated the extent to which companies impact our world, and our world can impact companies. Ignoring customers, advocacy groups, and other stakeholders is no longer an option. Develop a clear picture of where your organization stands in relation to climate but do not stop there. Cast your net wider. Take this opportunity to tell a coherent story about your place in the world. This way, you'll never have to scramble to formulate a half-baked response to the next wave of social activism. Who knows, you may even lead the next great movement.

# CHAPTER 7

# Partner With Stakeholders

The executives, board members, and employees of large companies feel besieged from all angles: Popular discourse portrays their businesses as the enemy and the root cause of climate change, along with many other societal evils. Regulators inundate them with new restrictions, and countless nonprofits, regulatory bodies, and interest groups demand they cut—if not completely eliminate—greenhouse gas emissions. Drastically shifting consumer preferences and investor expectations prompt them to adapt in seemingly endless ways. They are in dire need of climate clarity and guidance on what climate change means for their companies and what they should do.

The most successful businesses today understand that the boundary between a company and the rest of the world is more permeable than ever before. And, as much as one organization can do to create change, real change often requires collaboration with a wide range of stakeholders. These are parties that are affected by or can affect your business, from regulators to shareholders to employees. Such partnerships can present unique opportunities that not only combat climate change and avoid its associated risks but also grant you a competitive edge and a stronger connection with customers.

That being said, it's impossible to make everybody happy. At times, your values, strategies, and concerns may differ from those of a stakeholder to the point that a partnership is impossible. Even in those cases, however, you still need to maintain engagement. You can use the processes in this chapter to stay abreast of your stakeholders' concerns and keep lines of communication open. One day, they might offer some invaluable insight, or you might end up building coalitions around important issues. But before you can engage with your stakeholders, you first need to understand who they are and what they care about.

Stakeholders in a business are basically anyone who cares about or is affected by what the company does. Why do stakeholders even matter? Well, because they can all have a say in whether the company sinks or swims, and what the company does can come back to bite them too. Taking stakeholder opinions and concerns seriously can help companies spot and deal with potential problems before they blow up. For instance, tackling climate issues head-on can save a company from legal headaches or a hit to its reputation. Plus, stakeholders can be a gold mine of resources, such as money, talent, and new opportunities. Keeping those relationships sweet can open all kinds of doors for a company. When done right, stakeholder engagement sparks innovation and collaboration. When companies team up with stakeholders, they bring fresh ideas to the table, helping develop better climate solutions, stay ahead of the curve on upcoming climate regulations, dodge compliance issues down the road, and build trust in the community, giving companies a social license to operate—the green light to keep doing their thing without hassle. This is crucial for long-term success.

As with most things, there is a flip side. Engaging with stakeholders can mean additional scrutiny, often by people who have no idea about the intricacies of your business model or organizational dynamics. Entering the climate conversation will shine light on your company's actions—or lack thereof. When stakeholder expectations—whether realistic or not—are not met, things can get uncomfortable very quickly. Stakeholders may push you toward escalating climate commitments beyond what aligns with your company's strategic goals. And in some cases, stakeholder preferences can change as you go. So, you want to set yourself up for success by being thoughtful and selective before you even get into those conversations.

My prescription for all these potential ills is simple: focus on long-term value alignment. That means figuring out what your company stands for and sticking to it while also finding common ground with others. This way, you won't just be listening to the loudest voices but building genuine partnerships. Of course, you could take the box-checking approach, but here's what might happen: Things might seem rosy at first, but then you could face accusations of greenwashing. Plus, trying to keep up appearances can be tough in the long run.

## Know Your Stakeholders

The first step is to identify who your stakeholders are. Start with the question: Who is affected by my company's operations? Include both internal stakeholders (investors, employees, etc.) and external stakeholders (customers, government agencies, community, climate-focused non-government organizations (NGOs), industry organizations, suppliers, distributors, etc.). Next, think about everything you know about each groups' concerns and needs that could be related to climate. Make sure you record this information systematically—although the exact format is up to you. If your company has a market- or customer-research arm, I suggest mobilizing them to help with this task. If your company is smaller, talk to your customer-facing employees and tap into your own knowledge. If you have resources, conduct in-depth interviews, focus groups, or perhaps surveys with customers and community members, and review the published positions of NGOs and government agencies.

To make this information easily digestible, you can create a stakeholder map. A stakeholder map is a visible representation that identifies who the stakeholders are and shows how they are connected to your company/project, what they want, and how you will engage them. This can be as simple as a chart that indicates each stakeholder's degree of interest in your company's climate response and the level of formal power—or influence—they have over your decisions. At the end of this process, you will have an understanding of who your stakeholders are and how you will treat them. This is a common approach, and many companies already use stakeholder maps as a project management tool. While helit can help you avoid costly blind spots, it is not necessary, The bottom line is that some relationships you will manage closely, with a lot of back and forths, while with others you'll focus on keeping them satisfied without close engagement. Yet others will need to be kept informed throughout the process but without much tactical input.

Once you understand your stakeholders, you can begin to engage with them, whether that entails merely targeted communication or a full-blown partnership. Let's take a look at the key stakeholder types and engagement strategies for each.

# Internal Stakeholders

### Shareholders

Shareholders are individuals or groups who own a piece of your company. They're directly invested in how well it does financially, but their position on climate will vary. Some of them care a lot about climate, others not so much. Depending on how long they want to hold your company's stock, many are all about making quick money and boosting the stock price, even if it means neglecting long-term environmental consequences—or the company's risk exposure. For example, they might prioritize short-term profits from fossil fuel extraction over investing in renewable energy sources despite clean energy's long-term environmental and economic benefits.

When it comes to making decisions about the future of your company, shareholders can have a big say. Large institutional investors, such as pension funds, can exert influence to sway companies' policies toward climate. They can do so by voting for eco-friendly board members, proposing climate-friendly policies, or threatening to pull their investments from polluting companies. California Public Employees' Retirement System is an example of such high-profile stakeholder using its clout to nudge companies toward greener practices. They have been known to ditch investments in companies based on environmental concerns, even though divestment is usually attempted as the last resort. In the same manner, pension funds themselves can get in hot water with their own stakeholders.

There's a growing recognition—particularly among institutional shareholders—that climate change presents financial risks. Exposure to both acute and chronic climate risks—including extreme weather events, regulations, and consumer demands—can hit a company where it hurts—in the wallet. Some shareholders are looking ahead and urging companies to get ahead of the curve.

Now, we've got ESG ratings, most of which include climate-related metrics. They're like a quick peek into how sustainable a company is. Handy for shareholders who don't have time for deep dives, and that's often the majority. But, as discussed in Chapter 1, they are not foolproof. Different agencies might rate a company differently, and they might not catch everything. ESG ratings are a good starting point, but some shareholders aren't stopping there. They're doing their own homework and having direct conversations with companies about climate issues.

What does this all mean for you? First, make sure that you understand and keep track of the ESG reporting and ranking agencies' requirements to make sure you get credit for all the good work you are doing on climate. When interacting with more engaged shareholders, remember that climate is a learning experience for everyone. You can become a trusted partner in this exploration. Frame your arguments around long-term financial benefits and risk mitigation. Show how addressing climate change can improve the company's bottom line. Building a solid business case for your climate efforts will go a long way.

### Management

Management includes the folks calling the shots and keeping the company running smoothly. Their main goal is to hit the company's goals while making sure everyone involved stays happy. But here's the catch: Management and owners often aren't the same people. And that leads to what we call the "agency problem." This means there's a disconnect between what management wants and what the owners (shareholders) want, especially when dealing with climate change.

Managers' paychecks often depend on short-term success, like hitting quarterly profit targets. These key employees are incentivized to focus on making their numbers look good. Of course, making money is important, but maximizing short-term profit can be at odds with the long-term sustainability of the company. For example, investing in green tech or eco-friendly processes could mean taking a hit on immediate profits. It could also carry increased risks compared to business as usual. Shrewd managers often find ways to resist meaningful change by talking a big game about being eco-friendly but not really walking the walk. The game becomes all about looking good in the short term.

Tying management's bonuses to long-term sustainability goals can give them a reason to care about the planet beyond just making money today—we discussed it in Chapter 6. But more likely than not, those may be your colleagues or even seniors. Or this option may not be on the table or even appropriate for your company altogether. To win managers' support on climate issues, it's crucial to offer solutions rather than just pointing out problems. Present actionable proposals or potential steps the company can take to tackle climate concerns head-on. Additionally, it helps to demonstrate industry trends, showcasing how competitors are embracing climate action and the advantages they're gaining from it. Finally, keep a close eye on regulatory developments. This presents an opportunity to help management stay ahead of the curve by informing them of new regulations and explaining how they might impact the business.

### Employees

As generational change sweeps across workspaces in the United States, employees increasingly demand organizational change from their employers. Walkouts are only the most visible and most dramatic manifestation of this activist impulse. Inconsistent (or nonexistent) climate action leads masses of employees to become disillusioned with their employers. To prevent this disengagement, you need to take meaningful climate action. Decades of hollow marketing slogans about organic or "all-natural" products, "clean coal," and the abysmal environmental record of fast fashion companies have primed the public—and employees—to greet lavish climate commitments with skepticism. Any disconnect between what you say and what you do will leave you open to charges of greenwashing, which can sour your relationship with your employees and erode consumer trust.

To make sure that employees stay engaged, you need to hold everyone—especially upper management—accountable for the climate goals. Aim for total alignment so that everything you do and say reinforces and aligns with your commitments. In my experience, the best way to maintain this alignment is to maximize transparency and engagement across all layers of your organization. This allows everyone to see and celebrate the progress made, to understand how far they still need to go, and to know when individuals or teams don't hold up their end of the deal.

Let's be clear: Instilling organizational accountability requires serious changes. To make it happen, you need to make sure that everyone in the organization is on board. Otherwise, your efforts will fall flat. Engaging with employees requires building trust, so before anything else, you've got to lead by example. Without top-to-bottom accountability for results, progress is just wishful thinking, as discussed in Chapter 6. And trust me, employees can spot insincerity from a mile away.

Employee engagement is not a one-way street. As discussed in Chapter 4, you can activate your employees to identify and monitor climate risks. Get people talking. Organize chats, provide educational materials, and host workshops or discussions about climate change and its impact on your company—and their communities. Help your employees see the bigger picture and understand their role in making things right. Think of team events as a chance to weave climate-focused conversations into the fabric of your workplace. Provide employees with effective channels to have their voices heard and witness your responsiveness to what they bring up.

Listening to employees can be a game-changer in your climate readiness journey. Oliver Winter, CEO of a&o Hostels, knows this firsthand. He credits many of their best ideas for cutting carbon emissions to their workforce. By tapping into their insights, they've uncovered 175 actionable steps. According to Winter, when employees feel heard and valued, they're more motivated to take action. For instance, simple changes like sorting waste streams might seem like more work initially, but in the long run, they're cost-effective and environmentally friendly. A group of employees also zeroed in on Gaia, a dynamic carbon footprinting solution that provides detailed insights into the a&o's climate impact. The bottom line? Employee input can lead to innovative and effective solutions that benefit both the company and the planet.

You can also partner with employees to expand your company's impact. Arrange volunteer cleanups, tree plantings, or tours of green facilities—it's a win-win for team bonding and environmental awareness. Incentivizing eco-friendly behavior goes a long way. Offer rewards or recognition for things like using sustainable commuting options, cutting down on energy use, or getting involved in green initiatives. You may even consider giving employees a budget for their own sustainability projects; it empowers them to make a real difference. Create platforms where they can share tips for reducing their environmental footprint, both at work and home.

And, as with any change that you'd want to actually stick, make it easy for people to make green choices. Set up bike parking spaces, electric vehicle charging stations, or composting bins—whatever makes sustainability more convenient. Show them the benefits of going green —it's not just about saving the planet; it's about a healthier world, a better company image, and even potential cost savings. Make it personal. Talk about how climate action affects their well-being, from air quality to extreme weather events impacting their communities. And don't forget to celebrate their wins. Recognizing and cheering on their efforts in sustainability initiatives keeps the momentum going and inspires others to join in.

## External Stakeholders

### Customers

While every stakeholder matters, the most important stakeholders are your customers. Companies cannot exist without customers. In Chapter 3, we addressed ideas on how to influence customers and help them reduce their carbon footprint. But opportunities for engagement extend well beyond collaborating on climate action. Increasingly, customers crave brands that have an active, consistent social position. According to a report by the brand consultancy Lippincott, brands that deliver experiences of "progress" and "connection" grow as much as five times faster than brands that do not.[1] When you understand your customers and their priorities, you can communicate with them in an authentic way about climate change and any other social issue.

Such engagement can do wonders for your business. For example, Nike signed an endorsement deal with Colin Kaepernick in 2018 after the NFL ostracized him for taking a knee during the National Anthem as a demonstration of solidarity with Black Lives Matter. In the next three years, Nike's share price grew by 62 percent.[2] In 2020, the owner of Goya, a packaged foods producer, endorsed the Trump administration. Shortly after, their revenue spiked. In both cases, the companies weathered vicious social media backlash. But each knew their core audience and what that audience actually cared about. They took their stand, and it paid off.

The Internet brought about the end of the age of consumer ignorance. More than ever before, people have access to oodles of information, and businesses have less influence over the sources of that information—and misinformation. In a new crisis, customers will want to know what you're doing, where you're having success, and where you might be struggling. Obfuscation will only disenchant customers. In a recent report on corporate reputation by Porter Novelli, 78 percent of respondents agreed that "companies should have a point of view on environmental sustainability."[3] Nobody expects you to have all the answers right away. But they expect you to tr,; they expect you to track and share your progress, and, more than anything else, they expect you to be honest.

I invite you to drop any preconceived notions about your customers and actually look into where they stand on climate—and, more importantly, how their beliefs translate into their behavior. For example, there is a common portrayal of modern consumers as extremely sustainability-minded. According to a 2020 study by IBM and the National Retail Federation, 57 percent of surveyed consumers globally were willing to change their purchasing habits to help reduce negative environmental impact.[4]

But in reality, things are different. Take clothing. Fast fashion giants like H&M and Zara have been criticized for their unsustainable practices. Yet, in my experience, circular textile initiatives tend to hit a wall when they rely on a radical change in consumers' attitudes and behaviors. It is both consumer-centric and goes against the grain of how society has worked so far. Despite growing environmental consciousness, between 2000 and 2015, clothing production doubled, but the number of times an item of clothing was worn before being thrown away fell by over a third.[5] This is an outcome of a "green purchasing gap,"[6] in which consumers' buying behaviors do not fully match their positive attitudes toward sustainable products. Consumers are notorious for showing high interest in eco-friendly options when responding to surveys, but when faced with a price premium, they often choose cheaper, less sustainable options.

Of course, price matters when people actually spend money, especially when times are uncertain and money's tight. Plus, it's not always easy for consumers to figure out which products are eco-friendly or even find them in the first place. And let's be honest, sometimes they just won't care that much about climate. Make it your job to understand how wide the "green purchasing gap" really is for your company's customers—and what is at the core of it. What you find may surprise you. For example, in my experience when working with a retail clothing company, despite the team's desire to take the brand "to the next level" by focusing on articulating its sustainability and climate commitment, this was not a value its customers had prioritized in interviews and surveys. Instead, they were craving function, variety, and a sense of community. Given the nature of the garments the company sold, customer loyalty was predicated on trust and support rather than on environmental stewardship. There are no right or wrong answers here, only choices that you need to make to keep your customer engagement aligned with your company's strategy and positioning.

Once you know how your customers feel about climate change, you can make quick adjustments in behavior to capitalize on their (often shifting) views. When selling directly to consumers, consider offering incentives and promotions on eco-friendly products and services and campaigns that highlight steps you've taken to reduce your climate impact. If you sell products or provide services to other businesses,

sooner or later your clients will ask you to report your carbon footprint as part of their own climate reporting. For example, one midsize professional services company I worked with considered publicly
disclosing its climate metrics only when its leadership noticed that,
in an industry heavily impacted by emissions regulations, many of
their clients strongly suggested, and some started to require, that their
vendors provide this information.

Overall, while it's a bit complicated, it's clear that more and more
people are considering the environment when they shop. As companies
step up to showcase their green efforts and make eco-products more
accessible, we're inching toward a greener future. It's all about highlight-
ing the practical perks of going green, making climate-friendly products
affordable and easy to get, and even nudging folks along through social
influence. As a company, it's crucial to have your own perspective
and avoid jumping onto every political bandwagon. Steering clear of
pledging allegiance to any one political party or movement of the day
ensures your company's stance remains solid and inclusive, on par with
your mission.

### Suppliers

It is impossible to imagine a company that does not have suppliers.
They provide raw materials, goods, or services needed to keep your
company running. In Chapter 3, we discussed the opportunities and
pitfalls of engaging with suppliers from the perspective of climate action.
To maximize your and your suppliers' combined impact, you can start
by introducing carbon footprint reporting and reduction requirements
into your company's supplier code of conduct. You can also incorpo-
rate climate considerations into the supplier selection process and offer
incentives to nudge suppliers toward climate-friendly practices.

Implementing new practices or technologies can require significant
investment and a real financial burden for suppliers. They might scratch
their heads over whether going green will actually pay off in the long
run. Smaller companies might not have the working capital to comfort-
ably cover the upfront costs. Plus, smaller suppliers might not have
access to the technical know-how needed to comply with your climate

requirements. In fact, they might not have a clue about implementing and using new low-carbon tools or processes. And let's not forget reporting requirements: Gathering data on emissions and environmental impact can be outright daunting. If that is so for your company, you can bet it is for your mom-and-pop supplier. Some suppliers understandably worry that buyers like you might kick them to the curb if they can't keep up with the green trend. And given their limited negotiating power, smaller suppliers might just nod along with whatever your company says, even if it feels unfair—or unrealistic.

There are a few things you can do to alleviate these concerns. First, you could offer technical support or link suppliers with resources to guide them in adopting climate-friendly practices. Do not expect them to be able to fly a spaceship when all they have ever driven is a bicycle. Be ready to provide help to those who need it. Next, focus on building their capacity by providing workshops, training sessions, or sharing knowledge on sustainable practices and relevant regulations. Make reporting easier on suppliers by developing standardized templates or tools for them to use, simplifying data collection and reporting. Consider setting up recognition and reward programs to publicly applaud and incentivize suppliers who make significant strides in cutting emissions. But none of these will make much of a difference if you don't see your supplier engagement as a long-term team effort toward common goals rather than just a short-term business transaction. Ultimately, for collaborative climate action to be profitable, it has to happen within the long-term strategic context. If you expect commitment from others, be ready to first commit yourself.

### Investors and Lenders

Let's talk about two groups of individuals or organizations that can give your company money: lenders and investors.

Lenders are the banks or financial institutions that provide loans or credit to the company. They have an interest in the company's financial health to ensure repayment of their loans, which climate change can impact in a few important ways. First, there's the financial risk—like the costs of switching to eco-friendly tech or dealing with extreme weather messing up operations. Then, there's the fear of future regulations, which could hit profits hard if a company isn't ready. Last, there's the concern about reputation—if a company doesn't handle climate change well, it could hurt its image and make it tough to get money or customers.

Investors, on the other hand, are individuals or entities that allocate capital with the expectation of generating a financial return. We discussed shareholders, who are a subset of investors, earlier in this chapter, but not all investors are shareholders. In fact, investors come in various forms, including individual investors who invest their personal savings, institutional investors such as pension funds and mutual funds which manage large sums of money on behalf of others, retail investors who trade securities for personal portfolios, accredited investors meeting specific financial requirements, venture capitalists and angel investors who fund startups, and mutual fund investors who pool money to invest in diversified portfolios. Unlike shareholders, investors may not necessarily have ownership rights or voting privileges in the companies they invest in, depending on the type of investment vehicle they choose.

Investors may have a long-term, strategic view of climate issues. Some institutional investors, in particular, will have a broad range of concerns regarding your company's response to climate change. They will expect you to keep a close eye on financial risks like stranded assets, potential supply chain disruptions, and regulatory uncertainties. For example, they will need to know if their investments risk bleeding money as extreme weather events or resource shortages disrupt supply chains. Beyond financial concerns, investors also consider the broader implications of climate change on your company's future. Being strategic and transparent about things, such as transition costs, innovation opportunities, and reputational risks, will help alleviate investor concerns.

When engaging with investors on climate change, focus on both short-term and long-term financial opportunities. Do not just dwell on the risks. Transitioning to a low-carbon model requires upfront expenses, and investors want companies to develop thoughtful and realistic transition plans and capitalize on climate innovation for long-term growth. Use business cases to illustrate how tackling climate change can lead to cost savings, open up new markets, and boost efficiency. Back up your claims with hard data to demonstrate the potential impact on the bottom line. Set clear, ambitious climate goals that align with industry standards and develop a solid action plan to achieve them. Stay informed and proactive. Consider attending events focused on sustainable investing, participate in investor initiatives related to climate change, and be prepared to answer tough questions about your strategy.

A separate group worthy of attention is climate tech investors, that is, the individuals or entities who invest in technologies and solutions that fight climate change and support climate adaptation efforts. This includes venture capital and private equity firms, impact investors, family offices, corporate venture arms, or government initiatives. These investors look for opportunities to support startups and companies with innovative solutions to reduce GHG emissions or adapt to the impacts of climate change. Climate tech investors tend to be passionate about investing in-line with their values, and their focus is on both financial returns and impact outcomes. If you ever find yourself pitching climate tech solutions to investors, focus on their scalability and financial viability. Global issues require high-impact solutions, so make sure your product or service fits the bill.

### Environmental Nonprofits

Steering clear of NGO campaign target lists is usually the immediate goal of engaging with environmental nonprofits—no one wants to be the focus of nonprofit campaigns. But partnering with these organizations on climate-related issues can solidify your position as a market leader and influence the global, national, and local conversations around climate. For example, the World Green Building Council (WGBC) is working with dozens of national governments to develop zero-carbon standards. This is done in close consultation with over a hundred design, construction, and real estate management companies that are signatories to its Advance to Net Zero program. Some of these firms have had the opportunity to showcase their climate achievements for WGBC's vast global audience.

Nonprofits have been key drivers in the climate conversation—and particularly in discussions surrounding the responsibility of companies and businesses in contributing to climate change and the actions they should take. This dialog includes academic and nonprofit perspectives, often emphasizing what companies ought to be doing—engaging in commendable yet potentially expensive initiatives. This is why there has been a disconnect between the nonprofit and business worlds, a disconnect that some organizations are working to overcome. For example, the World Business Council for Sustainable Development is a global network of businesses driving sustainability leadership, focusing on solutions that are both environmentally sound and profitable. We Mean Business Coalition is another important global nonprofit working with some of the world's most influential businesses to accelerate action on climate change, while SME Climate Hub[7] specifically focuses on assisting small- and medium-sized companies in taking climate action. And, of course, there are countless national and regional nonprofits, climate-focused centers and institutes at universities, and even influential local organizations.

This means that you may very likely find yourself in a position where you have to make decisions about allocating your time and resources. I recommend doing your homework on the key players and ranking them based on a few criteria. You want to partner with reputable, influential organizations—this can extend the reach of your initiatives and enhance their impact. Consider your company's potential to influence specific nonprofits. You deserve to be heard. Healthy relationships—in business and life—should be mutually beneficial, so look for organizations that are open to collaboration. Finally, consider their potential to impact your business, whether directly or indirectly.

Why engage with nonprofits in the first place? Besides the obvious reputational benefits, it's essential to embrace diverse perspectives, including critical ones, which climate nonprofits will provide with gusto. Nonprofits can be incredible thought partners—especially in emerging markets and can lend credibility to your efforts to implement innovative climate solutions. Just make sure to prioritize organizations that align with the company's core values and goals.

## Regulators

Staying abreast of changing climate regulations and laws is tough—yet fundamental to your company's success. Yet there is more to engaging with regulatory agencies than assessing your company's compliance with emission standards or obtaining permits for emissions-reducing projects. In the past, corporations could get away with sending lobbyists to kill any sort of climate legislation that popped up. That strategy has become embarrassingly obsolete. Instead, focus on building meaningful relationships with regulators. Invite regulators to talk to your employees and leadership, so they can articulate their position on climate change policy. Then, make suggestions about upcoming legislation and rules to make sure that future regulations mitigate climate change without completely destroying your business model. This is your opportunity to shape local, regional, and perhaps even national policies for a fair low-carbon economy. Legal experts and consultants could be extremely helpful in helping you navigate such high-stakes relationships.

One of my clients suggested tweaks to a specific GHG emission regulation that made sure that the new regulation didn't create harmful conflicts with existing laws. In addition, the client suggested piloting new science-based emissions permitting structures before rolling them out nationwide to make sure that the legislation would have the intended impact without causing significant unforeseen operational difficulties. Such a close relationship offers two main benefits. First, it gives you input into upcoming regulations, and second, even if you can't impact the regulation, you will at least know what to expect, often earlier than competitors which haven't fostered the same rela- tionships. While only part of my client's recommendations ended up being reflected in the final version, this move cemented the company's reputation as an industry leader. There are, of course, limits to this approach. Regulators have a job to do, and they ultimately have the final say. You won't have much success if all your suggestions focus on gutting the new regulations.

Engaging with regulators can yield additional, tangible benefits, particularly as regulations evolve and new funding opportunities emerge. For instance, green bonds are becoming increasingly available as various jurisdictions enact regulations to promote sustainability. Many government entities have sustainable procurement policies prioritizing climate-friendly products and services, creating opportunities for small businesses in these sectors to target government contracts through local government green procurement programs. Keeping up-to-date with these regulatory developments can open doors to funding and business opportunities.

### Competitors and Industry Organizations

Partnering with competitors can be difficult, but a lack of industry consensus on climate strategy often leads to bad publicity, increased regulation, and loss of customers.[8] Industry-wide alliances, like Canada's Oil Sands Innovation Alliance (COSIA), can go a long way toward combating climate change while increasing profits. COSIA's 13-member energy companies collaborate to reduce the sector's waste, GHG emissions, and negative impacts on water and land. Their members have exchanged 560 technologies and innovations with a total investment value of $900 million,[9] including carbon capture, waste heat capture, and energy efficiency.[10] Consider developing climate standards with your competitors and partnering with them to spread the costs and speed up the change. Or join an industry association with climate change commitments.

As representatives of business, associations understand the issues that are essential to their members. As such, these associations are well-placed to provide advice and guidance on climate issues through the development of tools and the dissemination of best practices. There are even cross-industry business organizations focused on helping companies solve a specific set of challenges. For example, the Renewable Energy Buyers Alliance includes large companies collaborating on renewable energy procurement, sharing best practices, and driving market demand for clean energy.

To make the most of collaboration with other industry players, you would be wise to support initiatives that unite investors, companies, and environmental groups to establish common standards for climate-conscious business practices. Advocate for industry-specific benchmarks to measure climate risks and promote climate readiness, enabling shareholders to compare companies within their sectors and recognize leaders. Industry associations can be your ally in engaging policy makers to promote policies that support climate action while benefitting your bottom line.

### Communities

Most companies care about their communities. From neighborhood breweries to headquarter offices of corporate behemoths, each year, companies of all sizes participate in countless river cleanups, food drives, or used clothes collection events. Yet, too often, companies overlook the community needs related to climate change.

Before you execute your climate strategy, work to understand how climate change will impact the community and then do everything possible to mitigate the negative environmental, social, and health impacts of your actions. Despite being indirect, they are real. Support local nonprofits, government and civic organizations, and educational institutions. For example, Google.org's Impact Challenge on Climate distributes funds to local organizations, including Climate Farmers in Germany and Snowchange Cooperative, a Finnish organization committed to "rewilding landscapes in the European North."[11] One global technology company asked me to help them better understand how climate and broader sustainability concerns by community members can impact the fate of their data center development projects. Using this information, we then worked on strengthening the business case for community investment.

As you start talking to people in your communities, you will discover the complex web of their needs and concerns, with climate only part of the whole picture. In the words of George Bundy Jr., a global thought leader in sustainability and Chief Sustainability Officer at Darling Fibers,

> I have a challenge with the way that we look at individuals' responsibilities to address those [climate—V.F.] needs without educating them around why it's important. It's important to someone in Oakland who's got a food desert and doesn't have any access to fresh food. You ask them to buy an LED bulb to help reduce climate change, and they're looking at you like, 'Can I get fresh food first?'

Indeed the changing climate is not the only challenge to today's communities. There are chronic issues like access to quality health care, missing economic opportunity, public safety, and such perennial environmental concerns like pollution, waste management, access to green spaces, or access to clean water.

Climate change can often act as a multiplier of existing challenges. Economic disparity can make some communities less prepared to handle the financial burdens of climate disasters. Similarly, inadequate health care infrastructure can be overwhelmed by the health impacts of climate change. You may come face to face with the impacts of climate change exacerbating existing economic inequalities and pushing low-income communities further into poverty. Shifts in rainfall patterns disrupt agricultural production, resulting in food insecurity and intensifying competition over scarce resources, social unrest, and conflict. The list can go on and on.

You get to choose the role you'd like to play in your communities. Just remember that climate change will impact not only where your headquarters are located but also the locations of communities that are homes to your supply chain partners, their workforces, and even where your consumers live. Jochen Hauff, Director of Corporate Strategy, Energy Policy, and Sustainability at BayWa r.e. AG, says it best:

> Adaptation is not only about construction in urban centers. The focus needs to be on regenerating our rural ecosystems, most notably in agriculture and forestry.... People living in

rural areas will and have to benefit directly from the investment and improved value creation through renewable energy and adaptation measures.... The disparity of incomes and available services versus urban centers needs to be reduced. This can reduce frustration and polarization and help a political stabilization which we need, in turn, for investment coming in. A virtuous circle, once in motion.

So, in a nutshell, teaming up with others isn't just a feel-good move; it's an essential strategic play to avoid problems, shape policies, and boost both reputation and business opportunities.

# CHAPTER 8

# Survive This Sea Change and the Next

In the early 20th century, some companies hired "VPs of electricity" to deal with the arduous task of bringing electric power to their offices. Someone needed to pull the cords and install and manage the mysterious boxes called "transformers," all of which required arcane expertise, if not outright wizardry.[1] When electricity was first brought to the White House, they had an electric specialist to turn on the lights because President Harrison and the First Lady were scared of doing it.[2] The situation didn't last long, and the task of running electricity to buildings soon became commonplace. If you follow the advice in this book, soon your company will treat climate readiness programs the same way it does electricity. It will become second nature, so integrated into the business that you hardly notice it.

Then, new crises will arise, and we'll have to adapt again. The world brings up one disruption after another: 2020 began as a year of climate for corporate strategists but quickly turned into the year of COVID-19. Then, in the United States, in the wake of the massive Black Lives Matter protests, 2020 became the year of diversity, equity, and inclusion (DEI), only for the political pendulum to swing away from it by late 2024. Economic volatility was followed by unrest and instability globally. As a leader, you may be wondering about the challenges around the broader sustainability agenda, automation, cybersecurity, and the seismic shifts surrounding remote and hybrid workplaces.

Each of these shifts presents unique challenges. For all of them, it is easy to get lost in the details and overwhelmed by the crush of different opinions and new information. Add to that the day-to-day challenges of making sure that a business runs smoothly, and it's no surprise that companies struggle to respond quickly to problems as they arise. And when they do respond, it's often surface level, as the sheer amount of uncertainty and range of issues overwhelm decision makers. Just as with electricity, to be effective, your response to disruption needs to integrate a new way of thinking.

With any transformation, it is impossible to take into account every scrap of data and each bit of nuance. But certain tenets that make up a transformation philosophy can serve as a guiding light, helping you focus on what's essential. You can use these to help in the climate transformation journey and to address the next sea change that will inevitably occur.

## Take It Personally

During the writing of this book, my then-home state of Maryland went from United States Department of Agriculture (USDA) hardiness zone 7b to 8a. Curiously, my fellow gardeners in the "Dirty Annapolis" Facebook group were mostly happy. Dahlias and gladioli could now overwinter there, which meant we didn't need to dig them up every fall. Yet others recognized that this shift is but a harbinger of things to come.

Climate conversation is seemingly everywhere, but it's a proxy for much deeper shifts. It has us reconsider our relationship with ourselves, the environment, and society as a whole. Climate change serves as a profound allegory for the existential tightrope we walk. It is not merely an environmental challenge but also an economic, social, and moral one.

Achieving climate readiness—whether at the level of a company, community, nation, or the entire world—requires a personal transformation. It's about redefining our expectations, both of others and of ourselves. This isn't the time for small-mindedness. The challenges ahead call for evolution. We unavoidably confront questions of identity—who do we aspire to be in the face of these challenges? Can we rise to the occasion? It's about reassessing priorities and recognizing that while you might postpone this transformation, you can't sidestep it indefinitely.

To thrive in the present and shape the future, we must align ourselves accordingly. We must become a force capable of addressing the needs of the present—and meeting the future head-on. The undeniable acceleration of change in key areas of life requires greater agility, ingenuity, and determination than ever before. So, ask yourself: "Who do I need to become to build the economy of tomorrow?"

I know that this is a lot to ask. I am not a denier of the infamous "human nature" that tends to interfere with and often negate the best-laid plans and vivid dreams for the bright future of humanity. It's easy to lose hope and faith in the ability of human beings to better themselves. In today's world, we are mired in distractions, falling into decision fatigue, and sometimes too overstimulated to react appropriately to the rapidly changing world. I am clear that the transformation I am talking about here is neither easy nor simple. But it is what's required to integrate all you have learned from the climate readiness journey and to ensure the organizational changes you've made stick.

Business is one of the most personal things in which one can engage. Ultimately, it is a reflection of you and the world you want to live in. I know that this book so far may have read like an elaborate, never-ending to-do list. We're nearing the end of an era where companies could get away with merely appearing green. All around us, greenwashed narratives are collapsing because they lack the authenticity that the world so desperately craves. But the solution isn't to curtail climate efforts; that would be a step backward. We need to move forward and build a new foundation for our relationship with each other and with nature. It's time to shift your focus—from merely ticking boxes to embarking on a meaningful, transformative journey.

I know you care about making a difference. Otherwise, you wouldn't read this book. My goal is to equip you with the tools you need to drive real change. But you and only you can breathe life into each step on your company's climate journey. Only you can inspire and lead others. Only you can transform the very core of your business to begin building a truly sustainable regenerative economy. We already have the tools; we just need to pay attention to what's possible and seize the opportunity to go further. Instead of viewing climate readiness as a mere cost center, see it as the backbone of your organization. If we are really paying attention to what's possible, we can go far.

## Choose Your Role

The story about the VP of electricity may sound quaint—if not outright anachronistic. After all, what relevance can it hold to the dilemmas of the 21st century? But if you think about it, organizations installing C-level executives in emerging high-priority areas are following a similar pattern of corporate behavior. Think about your company's Chief Sustainability Officer, if it has one, or its Chief Digital Officer, or its Chief Impact Officer. Such titles don't have to be fancy—in a smaller organization, the same responsibilities could fall on a line manager "coordinator" or perhaps a volunteer "sustainability committee." These functions are all the signs of changing times—and shifting organizational focus. They are necessary now, and some will stick around for a long time; others will get absorbed into the organizational DNA, yet others will be completely forgotten.

If you are your company's sustainability leader, this means that, eventually, your job might not be a thing anymore. Maybe you're already feeling like you're boxed in. With everyone realizing how crucial certain things are (think "electricity" level crucial), you've got a decision to make: You have a choice—get stuck in organizational turf battles, or get ahead of the curve and lead the way. If you're managing sustainability efforts for your company, you have a choice to make: Who do you have to be to succeed in your mission beyond just scratching the surface into just a cost center? Bad move. That's the fast track to getting tangled up in a competition you don't want, a competition in which it's all about who's got the best ratings.

And it all comes down to a simple choice. You can choose to be an agent of change. If you are a company leader, what is the future that you are building for your team, your customers, or your partners? If you are a business owner, how does your company's climate resilience support the legacy you are creating? If you are a sustainability manager, how are you contributing to the transformation of your company? If you are a consultant, are you in the business of repackaging yesterday's insights—or are you laser-focused on crafting real, innovative, sustainable solutions?

Throughout this book, we've explored numerous decision points at which you have been called to choose one course of action over another. Often, we perceive choice as a spectrum of possibilities and varying degrees of freedom. But reality tells a different story. Real-life choices tend to be severely reduced by limited information, power dynamics, deadlines, and financial constraints. At any moment in time, it may feel like you have only one option, a Hobson's choice of sorts, where you either take it or leave it. It can seem like an impossible decision, but, in truth, most of the time, choice works this way. That's life.

Despite distractions, uncertainties, and setbacks on their climate readiness journeys, leaders across companies similar to yours have shown tremendous courage, vision, and tenacity. They have made different choices around their goals, approaches, and specific climate actions. Some of their efforts have been less successful than desired, and they deeply understand the complexities of the challenges they face. But they all have made a profound choice to respond to climate change by stepping into their own leadership, to forge a path to a new future for their organizations.

## Focus on What Matters Most

The true value in compiling, analyzing, and reporting any sort of data can only be realized when efforts are focused on issues that matter most. As you navigate the utterly unpredictable future, you need a structured way to think about not just what to do about climate readiness but also why to do it. Throughout the chapters of this book, you have been presented with somewhat of a menu of options for handling the challenges to your company as a result of the changing climate, regulatory environments, and stakeholder preferences. This can be overwhelming in and of itself. Add to it other challenges that invariably affect your company. Depending on your location and industry, these can be anything from urbanization, continuing environmental degradation, geopolitical calamities, emerging ethical quandaries, deep ideological divides, and increasingly agitated social wounds. All of these are on top of the fundamental need to keep the lights on and turn a profit.

One way to bring some measure of certainty into this utterly uncertain decision landscape is to find alignment along the values continuum. The concept is not new: Many leadership thought leaders emphasize the importance of core values in guiding decision making, especially during uncertain times. Core values act as a guiding light, providing consistency and direction when faced with unfamiliar situations. Aligning your actions with a core set of values can be the recipe for sanity for your entire organization.

On a base level, maximizing shareholder returns can be the single core value for your organization if you so choose. Despite common misconceptions, this would not mean that you shun considering climate change in your decisions. Review Chapter 7 to better understand the concerns of your shareholders and investors. Everything you do will be seen through the lens of profit and loss, and making a solid business case will be vital. You will be wise to focus on climate risks. Pursue opportunities that deliver clearly observable—if not immediate—monetary value. While this "profit-first" approach is common—and valid—many companies attempt to balance it with a broader, impact-oriented one by integrating nonmonetary benefits into their business decision-making logic. I'll leave it up to you to decide exactly how much to care. But in choosing areas to apply your attention and efforts, it helps to refer to some sort of a commonly accepted framework.

One such set of core values is presented in the Earth Charter.[3] Created as an outcome of conversations during the 1992 Rio Earth Summit, the Earth Charter contains key ethical principles for fostering a sustainable global community. It connects issues surrounding environmental protection, human rights, and peaceful coexistence in a single ethical framework.

The Earth Charter is a holistic document with an ecological foundation. Some of its cornerstone concepts include ecological integrity and "respect and care for the community of life."[4] It declares that "every form of life has value regardless of its worth to human beings."[5] Addressing inherently "human" issues such as poverty, social and economic justice, democracy, and peace, it emphasizes the need to live within the ecological limits of the planet. Yet the Earth Charter is full of optimism. A fundamental assertion of the "inherent dignity of all human beings" and faith in human potential allows it to offer a compelling vision of a bright future of the humanity. Instead of solely focusing on the doom and gloom of current social and environmental issues, the Earth Charter seeks to promote a "joyful celebration of life."[6]

The Charter's principles can serve as a north star for just about anyone—from individuals to organizations and even national governments. To develop a comprehensive impact strategy in alignment with the Earth Charter, you will need to translate its general principles into more tangible approaches and actionable steps that make sense within the context of your business. Think about—and consult with your stakeholders—what each of these principles means for your company and your community. If your company were to take action on any of these principles, which areas of the business would be involved? How would you define and measure success?

For something more readily put into action, consider aligning your strategy to the United Nations Sustainable Development Goals (SDGs), a set of 17 interconnected objectives designed to address global challenges and improve the well-being of people and the planet.[7] SDG 13, Climate Action, zeroes in on addressing climate change and its impacts. Other SDGs address a wide range of issues, including poverty, hunger, health, education, gender equality, clean water, and more. The SDGs emphasize the importance of collaboration and partnerships between governments, businesses, civil society, and individuals to achieve the desired outcomes.

You may have seen SDGs prominently featured on companies' websites. By aligning their operations with these goals, businesses telegraph not only their general commitment to sustainability and social impact but also the key areas of focus. The goal of publicly aligning with the SDGs is to enhance brand reputation, appeal to ESG investors, attract or retain increasingly sustainability-minded customers, and gain a competitive edge in the market. The authenticity of such SDG alignment varies greatly, with companies exhibiting everything from deep commitment to mere lip service. Some are launching specific initiatives and projects directly aimed at addressing SDG targets. Others struggle to develop SDG-aligned goals and key performance indicators (KPIs) for their impact efforts in the first place. And many make broad commitments to the SDGs without specifying which goals they are prioritizing or how they plan to contribute.

When taken seriously, SDGs can provide a helpful framework for defining and prioritizing areas of impact and even channeling your company's innovation efforts. Each goal is accompanied by specific targets and indicators to measure progress. Keep in mind that the goals and indicators are formulated at the global level and are more appropriate for national- or subnational-level bodies than private enterprises. You will need to clearly and realistically establish your areas of responsibility and "translate" desired impacts and metrics into business terms. Also, the number of indicators can be dizzingly high (231 suggested by the UN Statistical Commission[8]), so choose your SDGs wisely or you risk drowning in data. In my experience, even the largest, most advanced organizations often struggle to define the "theory of change" behind their sustainability and impact investments, and to connect them not only to specific SGDs but also to the company's own mission, vision, priorities, and operational context.

This is why any company developing a sustainability strategy should start with a materiality assessment, a process through which it can identify and prioritize those aspects that matter most to the company itself, its employees, customers, community, and other stakeholders from economic, environmental, and social perspectives. With the scope of potentially relevant issues constantly expanding, you need to have a solid framework to focus activities around themes that make a real difference for the company—and the world. A materiality assessment is especially important for smaller companies because it allows them to focus their limited resources on truly critical issues, can support their business goals, and is feasible from an implementation standpoint. If you are interested in taking this step, the Global Reporting Initiative has a detailed guide on how to conduct a materiality assessment.[9] When done right, this assessment is not only an effective tool to bring your organization into focus, build alliances, and put your stake in the ground on issues of importance to your company, but a great way to focus your energy and define your company's very relationship with the world.

## Evolve Your Strategy

Corporate strategy failure to deliver expected outcomes is a major issue companies face today. One poll found that only 2 percent of leaders are confident they will achieve 80 to 100 percent of their strategy's objectives.[10] As you can see, chances are that your fresh-off-the-press climate strategy and thoughtful decarbonization plan could very well become yet another casualty of the corporate world's perennial ability to snatch defeat from the jaws of victory. To succeed against these odds —and be ready to stare down future challenges, you need to transform your approach to business strategy itself.

It is common to think of strategy's failure to deliver results as a failure of execution. Sure, there are many things that can go wrong during implementation. But is the failure of strategy actually and primarily an implementation problem—or a problem within strategy itself? We tend to think of strategy development and implementation in a linear way, as one following the other. Implementation follows strategy. You can prepare for it, plan for continuity of effort, and ensure stakeholder buy-in early on; in other words, do all the great things suggested by myriad experts preaching the primacy of implementation. And yet, by the time you get to implementation, strategy is already obsolete. Given my observations of companies grappling with the increasing pace of climate developments, I hope you'll agree with me here.

You see, the way strategy is typically developed has some major flaws. It's often a relatively slow process, which means companies can't adapt quickly to changes in the market. Many strategists stay focused on internal factors while lacking depth in understanding the broader competitive market landscape. Chasing precision while missing on the constantly shifting big picture makes us make decisions based on precise yet faulty assumptions. Strategists' addiction to frameworks can result in overly simplistic approaches, failing to capture the complexities of emerging challenges, such as climate change—and many more to come.

Don't forget the lack of focus, alignment, accountability, and resources endemic in many organizations. All these shortcomings typically end up coming to a head and ultimately dealt with during implementation, by which time it's often too late to make significant adjustments. The current approach to strategy development is not a match for the rapidly changing world of today and tomorrow.

To prepare your organization for the upcoming storms, you need to change your approach to strategy development. First, it should be cyclical not linear. Many developments occur in parallel, and you need a way to iterate and integrate learnings close to real time. The strategy development process has to move fast, using automation to quickly grab data and find efficient ways to uncover market insights. Plus, your strategy should be integrated with an eye on stakeholder alignment from the outset and consider how everything in the organization fits together. Your strategy must be contextualized by drilling down into market data, checking out what's happening in other industries, and talking with customers to really understand what is happening across your company. You should be adept at looking ahead of the markets and figuring out what's real and what's just a passing trend. And keeping an ear to the ground with constant feedback from the frontline operations is essential.

Uncertainty can keep a business stuck. Be on the lookout for the next challenge or crisis, so you can begin to consider your response before your competition is even aware of it. Every difficulty presents myriad opportunities. The bigger the challenge, the bigger the opportunities. Making well-informed assumptions—even as they might need to be adjusted later—turns uncertainty into risk. Your job is to build a robust risk management system, adapt it to climate change, and then be ready to use it to run best, most likely, and worst-case scenarios of any challenge that arises.

Start by pinpointing uncertainties—think technological advancements and environmental regulations. Then, get imaginative. Develop hypothetical scenarios by mixing and matching these uncertainties in different ways. This is where many strategists make the mistake of assuming a straight-line "baseline" scenario continuing into the future. "Flatlining" revenue or cost projections are rarely questioned. But when it comes to climate readiness, assuming that things will stay the same is a profound mistake. Without action, climate risks will grow, and our environmental, social, economic, and political conditions will deteriorate. This decline, sadly, is our collective baseline.

The next step is key—analyze how each scenario could hit your business and come up with contingency plans. This approach isn't just an analytical exercise. Scenario planning boosts your strategic agility and helps you spot potential blind spots. It encourages creative problem-solving and holds the key to your adaptability in dynamic environments. Scenario planning could be as complex as advanced analytical models and as simple as a few bullets on the back of a napkin. No matter how formal or informal, it should become a habit of decision makers in your company. This way, you can adjust as needed and stay on top of whatever comes your way.

## Get Smarter

Regardless of where you are on your climate readiness journey, every once in a while you may need external help. Experts can offer tremendous value when facing a new challenge. And by now, there is no shortage of climate change consultants in all price categories. Some focus on developing climate strategies and decarbonization plans, identifying key climate risks, and integrating them into overall risk management systems. Others provide technical services—they can help you by crunching the numbers to understand climate impacts and forecast emissions across different business scenarios. Finally, you can always find someone to help you put your plans into action.[11]

Trouble is, companies tend to expect their consultants to literally or figuratively know it all, and when it comes to climate change, no one truly does. According to the research company Verdantix, "no one vendor can provide depth of service across the full spectrum of strategy, technical, and implementation pillars."[12] General strategy powerhouses have been infusing climate and sustainability into their traditional offerings while frantically acquiring specialized providers to fill technical gaps. Many of the more traditional climate and sustainability consultancies hatched in the early to mid-2000s are not business practitioners. As a result, they tend to rely on their deep understanding of reporting requirements or compilations of climate-focused best practices as reported by other companies. But they often have trouble with pinpointing the strategic shifts that will enable you to strengthen your company's market positioning or define the precise tactics you'll need to employ to be successful in your operational context. Engineering services and software solution providers launching their own consulting practices tend to lack the ability to bring broader strategic and organizational initiatives to execution. Narrow-focused subject-matter experts can deepen your understanding of their respective fields. Still, they may be less than helpful when the time comes for you to prioritize and implement sustainability initiatives. This is your prerogative—and your duty as a leader.

So don't take what the expert says as gospel. Don't let consultants implement or establish mission-critical systems. Challenge them, engage them in conversations, and insist that they break things down from your company's point of view. Challenge their notion of "best practices." In rapidly shifting conditions, there is no single "right" way to do things. Instead, gain insights from experts and use them to develop the solutions that work best for you.

You don't have to—and, in fact, cannot—know everything you need to develop and implement a climate readiness strategy. There's still a big need for targeted advice and expert knowledge. So, look to collaborate with those who can provide insights on the latest trends and help craft strategies. But be selective and maintain control of the overall strategy and implementation to ensure that ownership, accountability, and organizational alignment are built into every stage of the process. This entire process serves as a knowledge management exercise. Utilize your collaboration with experts to enhance your organization's knowledge base. Expand your comprehension not only of climate issues but also of other sustainability and business topics. It's an opportunity to refine existing skills or acquire new ones. Remember, nobody will fix your business model for you. Your role extends beyond mere reporting and project planning. It's about fostering internal alignment and growth, recognizing that there's no one-size-fits-all solution. Embrace the complexity of the task at hand; in a field as dynamic and intricate as climate change, every answer you find will inevitably lead to more questions. Approach it as an ongoing quest for knowledge and improvement.

Use your collaboration with experts to uplevel your organization's knowledge. Sharpen your existing skills or learn entirely new ones. But no one will fix your business model. Your job is much more involved than reporting and planning a few projects. They need to help you align internally. No one size fits all. In addressing something as dynamic, technically complex, and politically tinged as climate change, the answers you get may very well, in turn, open up new questions. Grow into the complicated stuff.

Don't forget valuable sources of expertise outside the glitzy world of consulting. There are professionals with practical experience leading organizations through a climate readiness transformation. There are massive volumes of information in training programs and webinars. There are platforms like Ubuntoo,[13] founded by sustainability veteran Peter Shelstrate, working to connect companies with the expertise, solutions, and innovations to take climate and broader sustainability initiatives from ideas to implementation. There are national and local programs offering training and certification for businesses committed to climate-friendly practices and various technical assistance programs. For example, the U.S. Environmental Protection Agency runs a free program to help small businesses comply with environmental regulations and identify opportunities for sustainable practices.[14]

And remember that, often, the best experts exist within your own organization. Frontline employees and process owners will know more about what makes your company tick than any outside expert. While experts can help reframe internal conversations, they will never know as much about your company as the people doing the work. Work to unlock the expertise of your workers. Solicit their thoughts and opinions—and make sure to distill and apply learnings. Remain in as much constant contact with them as you can, and you will be astonished by the organizational expertise and creative insights you find there.

## Choose Hope

Our response to climate change is, to a large degree, a reflection of our deepest fears and aspirations, a mirror to the contradictions within our very souls. The fervor that permeates the conversations around climate has its roots in our age-old dance with fear as we recognize our own fragility in the face of it. All the talk about impending environmental crises from the mid-20th century seems to have culminated in the prospect of catastrophic climate change—something big enough to drastically disrupt humanity's way of living if not to wipe it off the face of the Earth completely. Many grapple with the looming anxiety of a major catastrophe on the horizon and feelings of inadequacy to confront it.

Psychologists use the term "climate anxiety" to characterize this sense of impending doom, fueled in part by the increased media coverage of climate issues, including reports on extreme weather events, rising sea levels, and environmental degradation, which can be disquieting. Research indicates that younger generations may be especially vulnerable to climate anxiety, feeling they will inherit the consequences of climate change caused by previous generations. For instance, a study by the American Psychological Association discovered that nearly 48 percent of individuals aged 18 to 34 reported that climate concerns influence their daily lives.[15] Add to the mix the lingering impacts of the COVID-19 pandemic, economic uncertainty, and geopolitical tensions, and you have the perfect brew for serious societal malaise. Bad news sells.

As is inevitable among humans, climate change provides perfect grounds for all sorts of shaming, guilting, catastrophizing, outrage, and righteous indignation. These are understandable yet mostly unproductive reactions from the perspective of orchestrating lasting societal change. Our justifiable desire for control collides with the utter uncertainty in our shifting environments, both natural and social. The seeming futility of action gives way to societal fatigue. Mistrust starts creeping into the conversations surrounding climate. Despair, disillusionment, and depression set in, aggravated by our disconnect from the natural world.

This profound connection to our core emotions is part of the reason behind the heightened fervor surrounding climate issues. Inevitably, our collective fears make their way into the business world to shape the ways in which we perceive our partners, competitors, and customers. The ways in which we think about our company's strategic or competitive positioning. The way we choose to explain our company's trajectory. This is why risk management considerations tend to be a much easier sell than potential gain. We focus on managing our company's reputation to avoid embarrassment first—and forge a deeper connection with customers second. We spend more money on assuring compliance rather than creating actionable strategies.

There's nothing wrong with this approach, but it is not enough for those of us who still hold onto hopes of creating a better world and improving ourselves. We clearly see the need to respond to climate risks—but also opportunities to turn climate readiness into a source of value. Instead of solely avoiding excess costs, I invite you to take a more proactive approach to generating value through changing business models, envisioning beyond conventional boundaries, recognizing possibilities, or creating new revenue streams from existing offerings. Supporting your communities through the inevitable adaptation to changing climate. Influencing your industry to focus on innovative solutions and develop and cultivate new market spaces. Not many leaders understand what climate readiness actually means or how they can accomplish it. Even fewer can see how they can stay prepared for other upcoming changes. But these are all pieces of the same mental puzzle. The common thread running through these challenges is the need for leaders to be agile, decisive, and forward-thinking enough to lead their organizations through uncertain times. You have to be able to learn and invent rather than simply react.

This shift requires hope.

You've heard, I am sure, that "hope is not a strategy." That's true, but I am talking about informed hope here. As we have seen with climate, large-scale change can present both risks and opportunities. When the next crisis arrives, greet it as an opportunity for growth. Look to enter new markets, tap into new sources of revenue, or create new products and services in response to shifting societal needs. To capitalize on new opportunities, your organization needs to be able to foresee and understand changes—and respond to them quickly. This may lead you to adjust your logistics, find new suppliers, or even shift the location of your operations. Use the resilience and efficiency you develop now to act on opportunities in the future.

You, the reader, are the source for my unrelenting hope. By picking up this book, you took on solving one of the defining challenges of our time. You dared to look for ways to make the world work by illuminating the silver linings amidst the challenges we face. You have been willing to navigate through uncertainty and wade through technical jargon, conflicting viewpoints, and opaque language. With each step you take in pursuit of actionable, profitable solutions to the climate crisis, we emerge as allies. It is this collective effort, this shared journey that fills me with hope that, together, we are more than capable of overcoming any obstacle that lies ahead.

# Notes

## Introduction

1. United Nations Framework Convention on Climate Change, "Commitments to Net Zero Double in Less Than a Year."
2. Graham, "Net-Zero Emissions Targets Adopted by One-Fifth of World's Largest Companies."
3. Falk and Mendiluce, "The SME Climate Hub Expands Its Global Footprint."
4. Climate Action 100+, "Climate Action 100+ Net Zero Company Benchmark 2.0 2023 Results."
5. CDP, "World's Biggest Companies Face $1 Trillion in Climate Change Risks."
6. Carlin, *Forbes*.

## Chapter 1

1. Intergovernmental Panel on Climate Change, "Global Warming of 1.5°C."
2. U.S. Commodity Futures Trading Commission, "Managing Climate Risk in the U.S. Financial System."
3. Centopani, "Climate Change Puts $450B Worth of Homes at Risk by 2050."
4. Swiss Re Group, "World Economy Set to Lose Up to 18% GDP From Climate Change If No Action Taken, Reveals Swiss Re Institute's Stress-Test Analysis."
5. Dell et al., U.S. Global Change Research Program.
6. Centers for Disease Control and Prevention, U.S. Department of Health and Human Services.
7. Huntington, *Alt Energy Mag*.
8. Zhang et al., "Temperature Effects on Productivity and Factor Reallocation: Evidence From a Half Million Chinese Manufacturing Plants." 1–17.

9. Harris and Wei, *Business for Social Responsibility*.

10. Bolsover, Deutsche Welle.

11. FEMA, "Stay In Business After a Disaster by Planning Ahead."

12. CDP, "World's Biggest Companies Face $1 Trillion in Climate Change Risks."

13. Park and Noh, "Climate Change Risk and Cost of Capital."

14. Cuff, GreenBiz.

15. Millani, "The Role of CDP Disclosure to Improve Access to Capital."

16. Bekmagambetova, *Barron's*.

17. Holmes, LendingTree.

18. Griffin, CDP Worldwide.

19. Milliken, John, and Kerry, Reuters.

20. United States Environmental Protection Agency, EPA.gov.

21. Australian Government, Clean Energy Regulator.

22. Aylor, et al., Boston Consulting Group.

23. U.S. Securities and Exchange Commission, "SEC Announces Enforcement Task Force Focused on Climate and ESG Issues."

24. Flood, *Financial Times*.

25. Roach, "Top 50 Asset Managers Created Internal ESG Ratings."

26. BlackRock, "2020 TCFD Report."

27. Moody's, "Moody's 2019 Corporate Social Responsibility Report."

28. Smith, *Citi (blog)*.

29. Union of Concerned Scientists, "A Climate of Corporate Control."

30. Laville, "Top Oil Firms Spending Millions Lobbying to Block Climate Change Policies."

31. Greenpeace, "Exxon's Climate Denial History: A Timeline."

32. Cooper, "Corporate 'Greenwashing' Is an Even Worse Problem Given Climate Change."

33. Sabin Center for Climate Change Law, "Milieudefensie et al. v. Royal Dutch Shell plc."

34. Meijer, Reuters.

35. CDP Worldwide, "Celebrating CDP North America's 2020 A List."

36. Manfredi, "Alexander: Child of a Dream."

37. Simon. *The Ultimate Resource 2*.

38. Esser and Trayner, "CEOs Need to Grapple With Populist Backlash."

39. Riley, "100 Companies Responsible For 71% of Global Emissions."

40. European Commission, "2019 Assessment of the Progress Made by Member States Towards the National Energy Efficiency Targets for 2020 and Towards the Implementation of the Energy Efficiency Directive as Required by Article 24(3) of the Energy Efficiency Directive 2012/27/EU."

41. Carlin, "$100 Trillion Investment Opportunity in Climate Transformation."

42. Colak, Korkeamaki, and Meyer, "ESG and CEO Turnover."

## Chapter 2

1. U.S. Environmental Protection Agency (EPA), "Climate Change Indicators: Atmospheric Concentrations of Greenhouse Gases."

2. Intergovernmental Panel on Climate Change (IPCC), "Climate Change 2022. Mitigation of Climate Change. Summary for Policy Makers."

3. Greenhouse Gas Protocol, "Scope 3 Calculation Guidance."

4. CoolClimate Network, "Start With A Quick Carbon Footprint Estimate."

5. Greenhouse Gas Protocol, "Calculation Tools and Guidance."

6. Barnard, "Key Functionalities Reflected In The 2023 Carbon Management Software Green Quadrant Report."

7. Ember, "Carbon Price Tracker."

8. Hirst and Keep, "Carbon Price Floor (CPF) and The Price Support Mechanism."

9. Federal Office for the Environment FOEN, "Swiss Emissions Trading Registry."

10. Regional Greenhouse Gas Initiative (RGGI, Inc.), "RGGI 2022 Program Highlights."

11. Kruger, "Hedging an Uncertain Future: Internal Carbon Prices in the Electric Power Sector."

12. Center for Climate and Energy Solutions, "Internal Carbon Pricing."

13. Danone, "2019 Full-Year Results."

14. Carbon Pricing Leadership Coalition, "Report of the High-Level Commission on Carbon Prices."
15. Taylor and Skinner, "Global Corporate Survey 2023: Net Zero Budgets, Priorities and Tech Preferences."
16. NYC Accelerator, "LOCAL LAW 97."
17. International Renewable Energy Agency (IRENA), "Renewable Power Generation Costs in 2019."
18. US Department of Energy, "Better Buildings."
19. Silverstein, "Google Has Invested $3.5 Billion In Renewable Energy Projects Worldwide."
20. Duke Energy, "Duke Energy's $62 Million Solar Rebate Program Approved for North Carolina Residential, Business and Nonprofit Customers."
21. Energy For Everyone Propane, "The Future of Clean Energy—Today."
22. ClearSeas, "Marine Fuels: What Is Heavy Fuel Oil?"
23. U.S. Energy Information Administration, "Biomass Explained."
24. Hydrogen Council, "Why Hydrogen?"
25. International Energy Agency, "Combining Bioenergy With CCS."
26. IKEA, "Designing for a Circular Future."
27. Dell Technologies, "Accelerating the Circular Economy to Reduce Waste and Protect the Planet."
28. H&M Group, "Circularity."
29. Ridepanda.
30. Chevron, "Carbon C apture Helps Make a Lower Carbon Future Possible."
31. Climeworks.
32. Carbon Offset Guide.
33. Toffel and Macomber, "Building Climate—Resilient Cities and Infrastructure."
34. United Nations Framework Convention on Climate Change, "Commitments to Net Zero Double in Less Than a Year."
35. Threlfall, et al., "Towards Net Zero."
36. International Standards Organization (ISO), "IWA 42:2022(en) Net Zero Guidelines."

37. High-Level Expert Group on the Net Zero Emissions Commitments of Non-State Entities, "Integrity Matters: Net Zero Commitments by Businesses, Financial Institutions, Cities and Regions," 17.

38. Science Based Targets, "Set a Target."

39. Science Based Targets, "Companies Taking Action."

# Chapter 3

1. Toyota, "Vehicle Life Cycle Assessments."

2. Patagonia, "Introducing the New Footprint Chronicles on Patagonia.com."

3. BASF, "Eco-Efficiency Analysis."

4. European Commission, "Environmental Footprint Methods."

5. European Commission, "Ecodesign for Sustainable Products Regulation."

6. California Air Resources Board, "Low Carbon Fuel Standard Public Workshop: Concepts and Tools for Compliance Target Modeling."

7. International Standards Organization, "ISO 14044:2006 Environmental Management. Life Cycle Assessment."

8. Ecochain, "LCA Software for Business Users."

9. The Strategic Sourceror, "Walmart Rewarding Sustainable Suppliers With Better Financing From HSBC."

10. Danone, "Regenerative Agriculture."

11. Unilever, "Unilever Sustainable Agriculture Code."

12. BHP, "CDP Report—Climate Change 2023."

13. Hill, "Vodafone Embeds Environmental Criteria Into Its Supplier Selection Process."

14. Nellis, "Salesforce Acts on Climate, Requiring Suppliers to Set Carbon Goals."

15. Gutoskey, "How to Use Your Own Cup for Starbucks Drive-Thru and Mobile Orders."

16. Patagonia. WornWear.

17. The LEGO Group, "RePlay."

18. Nespresso, "Responsibility Meets Recyclability."

# Chapter 4

1. Shellenberger, *Apocalypse Never: Why Environmental Alarmism Hurts Us All.*
2. Scriven, *The Economist.*
3. Task Force on Climate-Related Financial Disclosures (TCFD), "TCFD Recommendations."
4. Sharma, Kumar, Vatta et al, "Impact of Recent Climate Change on Cotton and Soybean Yields in the Southeastern United States."
5. Task Force on Climate-Related Financial Disclosures (TCFD), "TCFD Recommendations."
6. Bousso, Meijer and Nasralla. *Shell Ordered to Deepen Carbon Cuts in Landmark Dutch Climate Case.*
7. Eisenstein, *Volkswagen Slapped With Largest Ever Fine for Automakers.*
8. Hotten, Volkswagen: The Scandal Explained.
9. Brangham and Dubnow, "Extreme Weather Causes Major Insurance Providers to Pull Coverage in California."
10. Kaufman, "Florida's Home Insurance Industry May Be Worse Than Anyone Realizes."
11. Shelton Group, "Ecopulse™ 2017 Special Report United We Understand."
12. Inter-American Development Bank (IDB), "The Most Unexpected Effect of Climate Change."
13. Maguire, "US Thermal Coal Exports Hit 5-year Highs and Top $5 Billion in 2023."
14. Perkins and Goliya, "Oil majors' Credit Ratings Under Threat From Growing Climate Risks: S&P Global."
15. Intergovernmental Panel on Climate Change, "Global Warming of 1.5°C."

# Chapter 5

1. CDP Climate Change 2023 Reporting Guidance.
2. United Nations Environmental Program (UNEP), "Resource Efficiency."
3. Henisz, Koller, and Nuttall, "Five Ways That ESG Creates Value."

4. We Mean Business Coalition, "The Climate Has Changed."

5. T. Whelan and C. Fink, "The Comprehensive Business Case for Sustainability."

6. GE, "GE Works: 2013 Annual Report."

7. Aeon, "Aeon Sustainability Data Book 2019."

8. M. Parker, "Letter to Shareholders."

9. T. Whelan and C. Fink, "The Comprehensive Business Case for Sustainability."

10. Unilever, "Our Climate Transition Action Plan."

11. Konrad, "Maersk Triple-E—A Detailed Look at the World's Biggest Ship."

12. Randall, "What Is Behind the Success of Electric Buses in the UK."

13. Coca-Cola, "What Is World Without Waste?"

14. Cruz Foam.

15. Ryor, "Shifting to Renewable Energy can Save U.S. Consumers Money."

16. Folk, "10 Ways Renewable Energy Can Save Businesses Money."

17. BloombergNEF, "The $7 Trillion a Year Needed to Hit Net-Zero Goal."

18. International Energy Agency (IEA), "Direct Air Capture."

19. Tesla, "Powerwall."

20. Airlock Insulation.

21. Barclays, "The Future of Food."

22. Reuters, "UK Supermarket Sainsbury's Launches EV Charging Business."

23. AECOM.

24. McMillin, *CNET Money*.

25. Crystal. *Israelis Sell Austria Snow*.

26. Poisson, "The ESG Data Revolution," 84.

27. The Rockefeller Foundation, *100 Resilient Cities*.

28. Stevenson, "Infrastructure Investment Trusts: A Long-Term Bet."

29. CDP, "Major Risk or Rosy Opportunity: Are Companies Ready for Climate Change?"

30. U.S. Department of Energy, "Solid-State Lighting Program."

31. Mollman, "Blockbuster 'laughed us out of the room,' Recalls Netflix Cofounder on Trying to Sell Company Now Worth Over $150 Billion for $50 Million."

32. Kuykendall. *S&P Global Market Intelligence.*

33. Egan, "Exxon Faces $20 Billion Hit from 'Epic Failure' of a Decade Ago."

34. Market Research Future, "Global Green Buildings Market Overview."

35. Emergen Research, "Sustainable Packaging Market Size, Share, Trends, by Materials (Plastic, Paper & Paperboard, Glass, Metal), by Packaging Type (Reusable Packaging, Recyclable Packaging, Degradable Packaging), by End Users (HealthCare, Food & Beverage, Personal Care, Others), Forecast to 2027."

36. Energy Global, " Renewable Energy Market Anticipated to Exceed US$1.5 Trillion by 2025."

# Chapter 6

1. Matsakis, "Thousands of Tech Workers Join Global Climate Change Strike."

2. Bergen and Day, "Big Tech Helps Big Oil Pump More, Belying Climate Pledges"

3. Pigou, "The Economics of Welfare."

4. European Environment Agency, "Internalisation of Externalities."

5. Pryor and Putti, "Carbon Pricing: Almost 25% of Emissions Now Covered Globally, but Coverage and Prices Must Rise Further."

6. Stokel-Walker, "Only Extreme Eco-Taxes on Flights Will Change our Flying Habits."

7. Tarbaton, "If Companies Want to Meet Climate Targets, They Must Take Employees on the Journey."

8. The Climate Registry.

9. Poisson, "The ESG Data Revolution," p. 29.

10. Ibid, 30.

# Chapter 7

1. Lippincott, "How to Grow When Markets Don't: Webinar Series Rewind."

2. Tamny, *Forbes*.

3. Novelli, "The Purpose Priorities Report: How to Respond in the New Era of Accountability."

4. National Retail Federation, "Meet the 2020 Consumers Driving Change."

5. Ellen MacArthur Foundation, "Circular Business Models, Redefining Growth for a Thriving Fashion Industry."

6. Johnstone and Tan, "Exploring the Gap Between Consumers' Green Rhetoric and Purchasing Behaviour," 311–328.

7. The Climate Hub.

8. Nurse, "2019 Top 10 Renewable Utilities—Solar and Wind Project Pipeline Analysis."

9. DiVito and Sharma, "Collaborating With Competitors to Advance Sustainability: A Guide for Managers."

10. Canada's Oil Sands Innovation Alliance, "Greenhouse Gases Management."

11. Google.org, "Google.org Impact Challenge on Climate 2020."

# Chapter 8

1. William A. Taylor. *What Every Engineer should know about Artificial Intelligence*.

2. The White House Historical Association. "When was Electricity First Installed at The White House?"

3. The Earth Charter.

4. Ibid.

5. Ibid.

6. The Earth Charter, "The Way Forward."

7. The Global Goals, "The 17 Goals."

8. Sustainable Development Goals, "SDG Indicators."

9. Global Reporting Initiative (GRI), "GRI 3: Material Topics 2021."

10. Bridges Consultancy, "20-Year Results From Surveying Strategy Implementation."

11. Taylor, Foyn and Skinner, "Green Quadrant: Climate Change Consultinting."

12. Ibid.

13. Ubuntoo, "We Use Collective Intelligence to Solve the Planet's Biggest Challenges."

14. U.S. Environmental Protection Agency (EPA), "Smart Steps to Sustainability 2.0."

15. Schreiber, "Addressing Climate Change Concerns in Practice."

# References

AECOM. n.d. Accessed April 22, 2024. https://aecom.com/.

Aeon. n.d. "Aeon Sustainability Data Book 2019." Accessed April 16, 2024. www.aeon.info/export/sites/default/common/images/en/environment/report/e_2019pdf/19_data_en_a4.pdf.

Airlock Insulation. n.d. Accessed April 30, 2024. https://airlock-insulation.com/.

Australian Government. n.d. "The NGER Scheme." *Website for Clean Energy Regulator.* Accessed July 20, 2021. www.cleanenergyregulator.gov.au/NGER.

Aylor, B., M. Gilbert, N. Lang, M. McAdoo, J. Oberg, C. Pieper, B. Sudmeijer, et al. 2020. "How an EU Carbon Border Tax Could Jolt World Trade." *Boston Consulting Group.* June 30, 2020. www.bcg.com/publications/2020/how-an-eu-carbon-border-tax-could-jolt-world-trade.

Barclays. 2021. "The Future of Food." May 4. https://home.barclays/news/2021/05/the-future-of-food/.

Barnard, A. 2023. "Key Functionalities Reflected in the 2023 Carbon Management Software Green Quadrant Report." *Verdantix.* December 7, 2023. www.verdantix.com/insights/blogs/key-functionalities-reflected-in-the-2023-carbon-management-software-green-quadrant-report.

BASF. n.d. "Eco-Efficiency Analysis." Accessed March 21, 2024. www.basf.com/us/en/who-we-are/sustainability/we-drive-sustainable-solutions/quantifying-sustainability/eco-efficiency-analysis.html.

Bekmagambetova, D. 2020. "Two-Thirds of North Americans Prefer Eco-Friendly Brands, Study Finds." *Barron's.* January 10, 2020. www.barrons.com/articles/two-thirds-of-north-americans-prefer-eco-friendly-brands-study-finds-51578661728.

Bergen, M. and M. Day. 2022. "Big Tech Helps Big Oil Pump More, Belying Climate Pledges." *Bloomberg.* August 16. www.bloomberg.com/news/articles/2022-08-16/microsoft-amazon-big-tech-help-big-oil-pump-more.

BHP. n.d. "CDP Report—Climate Change 2023."

BlackRock. n.d. "2020 TCFD Report." Accessed July 20, 2021. www.blackrock.com/corporate/literature/continuous-disclosure-and-important-information/tcfd-report-2020-blkinc.pdf.

BloombergNEF. 2022. "The $7 Trillion a Year Needed to Hit Net-Zero Goal." December 7. https://about.bnef.com/blog/the-7-trillion-a-year-needed-to-hit-net-zero-goal/.

Brangham, W. and S. Dubnow. 2023. "Extreme Weather Causes Major Insurance Providers to Pull Coverage in California." *PBS News Hour.* June 12. www.

pbs.org/newshour/show/extreme-weather-causes-major-insurance-providers-to-pull-coverage-in-california.

Bridges Consultancy. n.d. "20-Year Results From Surveying Strategy Implementation." Accessed April 8, 2024. www.bridgesconsultancy.com/wp-content/uploads/2016/10/20-Years-of-Strategy-Implementation-Research-2.pdf.

Carbon Pricing Leadership Coalition. 2017. *Report of the High-Level Commission on Carbon Prices*. Washington, DC: The World Bank. www.carbonpricingleadership.org/report-of-the-highlevel-commission-on-carbon-prices.

Bolsover. C. 2010. "Russia Begins Ban on Grain Exports After Fires Devastate Crops." *Deutsche Welle*. August 15. https://p.dw.com/p/Oo0X.

Bousso, R., B.H. Meijer., and S. Nasralla. 2021. "Shell Ordered to Deepen Carbon Cuts in Landmark Dutch Climate Case." May 26. www.reuters.com/business/sustainable-business/dutch-court-orders-shell-set-tougher-climate-targets-2021-05-26/.

California Air Resources Board. 2022. "Low Carbon Fuel Standard Public Workshop: Concepts and Tools for Compliance Target Modeling." November 9. www2.arb.ca.gov/sites/default/files/2022-11/LCFSPresentation.pdf.

Canada's Oil Sands Innovation Alliance. 2021. "Greenhouse Gases Management." Accessed July 20. https://cosia.ca/initiatives/greenhouse-gases.

Carbon Offset Guide. n.d. Accessed April 8, 2024. www.offsetguide.org/.

Carlin, D. 2021. "The $100 Trillion Investment Opportunity in the Climate Transformation." *Forbes,* June 2. www.forbes.com/sites/davidcarlin/2021/06/02/the-ieas-net-zero-climate-pathway-is-a-100-trillion-investment-opportunity/?sh=3e179c215597.

CDP Climate Change 2023 Reporting Guidance. n.d. https://guidance.cdp.net/en/guidance?cid=46&ctype=theme&idtype=ThemeID&incchild=1&microsite=0&otype=Guidance&tags=TAG-646%2CTAG-605%2CTAG-599%2CTAG-600%2CTAG-13145%2CTAG-13135%2CTAG-13140.

CDP. n.d. "Major Risk or Rosy Opportunity: Are Companies Ready for Climate Change?" Accessed February 3, 2024. www.cdp.net/en/research/global-reports/global-climate-change-report-2018/climate-report-risks-and-opportunities.

CDP. 2019. "World's Biggest Companies Face $1 Trillion in Climate Change Risks." June 4. www.cdp.net/en/articles/media/worlds-biggest-companies-face-1-trillion-in-climate-change-risks.

CDP Worldwide. n.d. "Celebrating CDP North America's 2020 A-List." *CDP website*. Accessed July 20, 2021. www.cdp.net/en/events/a-list-celebration.

Center for Climate and Energy Solutions. n.d. "Internal Carbon Pricing." Accessed July 20, 2021. www.c2es.org/content/internal-carbon-pricing/.

Centers for Disease Control and Prevention. n.d. "Impact of Climate on Workers." *U.S. Department of Health and Human Services.* Accessed July 21, 2021. www.cdc.gov/niosh/topics/climate/how.html.

Centopani. n.d. "Climate Change Puts $450B Worth of Homes at Risk by 2050."

Chevron. n.d. "Carbon C apture Helps Make a Lower Carbon Future Possible." Accessed April 6, 2024. www.chevron.com/what-we-do/technology-and-innovation/capturing-and-storing-carbon-emissions.

ClearSeas. n.d. "Marine Fuels: What is Heavy Fuel Oil?" Accessed April 5, 2024. https://clearseas.org/insights/marine-fuels-what-is-heavy-fuel-oil/.

Climate Action 100+. 2023. n.d. "Climate Action 100+ Net Zero Company Benchmark 2.0 2023 Results." www.climateaction100.org/wp-content/uploads/2023/10/2023-Key-Findings.pdf.

The Climate Hub. n.d. Accessed April 4, 2024. https://smeclimatehub.org/.

The Climate Registry. n.d. Accessed April 30. https://theclimateregistry.org/.

Climeworks. n.d. Accessed April 6, 2024. https://climeworks.com/.

Coca-Cola. n.d. "What Is World Without Waste?" Accessed April 30, 2024. www.coca-cola.com/us/en/about-us/faq/what-is-world-without-waste.

Colak, G., T. Korkeamaki., and N.O. Meyer. 2020. "ESG and CEO Turnover." *Proceedings of Paris December 2020 Finance Meeting EUROFIDAI-ESSEC,* October 13. Retrieved from Social Science Research Network. http://dx.doi.org/10.2139/ssrn.3710538.

CoolClimate Network. n.d. "Start With a Quick Carbon Footprint Estimate." Accessed April 8, 2024. https://coolclimate.berkeley.edu/business-calculator.

Cooper. n.d. "Corporate 'Greenwashing' Is an Even Worse Problem Given Climate Change."

Cruz Foam. n.d. Accessed April 15, 2024. www.cruzfoam.com/.

Crystal, M. 2009. "Israelis Sell Austria Snow." *Ynet News,* October 2. www.ynetnews.com/articles/0,7340,L-3782329,00.html.

Cuff, M. 2015. "Reporting Your Company's Carbon Footprint Can Save $1.5 Million a Year." *GreenBiz,* August 12. www.greenbiz.com/article/reporting-your-companys-carbon-footprint-can-save-15-million-year.

Danone. 2020. "2019 Full-Year Results." Press Release, February 26. www.danone.com/content/dam/danone-corp/danone-com/medias/medias-en/2020/corporatepressreleases/2019_danone_full_year_results.pdf.

Danone. n.d. "Regenerative Agriculture." Accessed April 30, 2024. www.danone.com/impact/planet/regenerative-agriculture.html.

Dell, J., S. Tierney, G. Franco, R. Newell, R. Richels, J. Weyent, and T. Wilbanks. n.d. "Energy Supply and Use." *2014 National Climate Assessment, U.S. Global Change Research Program.* Accessed July 20, 2021. https://nca2014.globalchange.gov/report/sectors/energy.

Dell Technologies. n.d. "Accelerating the Circular Economy to Reduce Waste and Protect the Planet." Accessed April 30, 2024. www.dell.com/en-us/dt/corporate/social-impact/advancing-sustainability/accelerating-the-circular-economy.htm#anchor.

Dr. Lor DiVito and Dr. Garima Sharma. 2016. "Collaborating With Competitors to Advance Sustainability: A Guide for Managers." Network for Business Sustainability. www.nbs.net.

Duke Energy. 2018. "Duke Energy's $62 Million Solar Rebate Program Approved for North Carolina Residential, Business and Nonprofit Customers." April 16, 2018. https://news.duke-energy.com/releases/duke-energy-s-62-million-solar-rebate-program-approved-for-north-carolina-residential-business-and-nonprofit-customers.

The Earth Charter. n.d. "The Way Forward." Accessed March 22, 2024. https://earthcharter.org/read-the-earth-charter/the-way-forward/.

The Earth Charter. n.d. Accessed March 22, 2024. https://earthcharter.org/.

Ecochain. n.d. "LCA Software for Business Users." Accessed April 8, 2024. https://ecochain.com/lca-software/.

Eisenstein, P.A. 2017. "Volkswagen Slapped With Largest Ever Fine for Automakers." *NBC News.* April 21, 2017. www.nbcnews.com/business/autos/judge-approves-largest-fine-u-s-history-volkswagen-n749406.

Egan, M. 2020. "Exxon Faces $20 Billion Hit from 'epic failure' of a Decade Ago." *CNN Business.* December 1. www.cnn.com/2020/12/01/business/exxon-oil-gas-writedown/index.html.

Ellen MacArthur Foundation. 2021. "Circular Business Models, Redefining Growth for a Thriving Fashion Industry." https://emf.thirdlight.com/link/circular-business-models-report/@/preview/1?o.

Emergen Research. n.d. "Sustainable Packaging Market Size, Share, Trends, By Materials (Plastic, Paper & Paperboard, Glass, Metal), By Packaging Type (Reusable Packaging, Recyclable Packaging, Degradable Packaging), By End Users (HealthCare, Food & Beverage, Personal Care, Others), Forecast to 2027." Accessed April 3, 2024. www.emergenresearch.com/industry-report/sustainable-packaging-market).

Energy For Everyone Propane. n.d. "The Future of Clean Energy—Today." Accessed April 8, 2024. https://propane.com/environment/.

Energy Global. n.d. " Renewable Energy Market Anticipated to Exceed US$1.5 Trillion by 2025." www.energyglobal.com/other-renewables/22082019/renewable-energy-market-anticipated-to-exceed-us15-trillion-by-2025/.

Ember. n.d. "Carbon Price Tracker." Accessed April 25, 2024. https://ember-climate.org/data/data-tools/carbon-price-viewer/.

Esser, V. and G. Trayner. n.d. "CEOs Need to Grapple With Populist Backlash."

European Commission. 2020. "2019 Assessment of the Progress Made by Member States Towards the National Energy Efficiency Targets for 2020 and

Towards the Implementation of the Energy Efficiency Directive as Required by Article 24(3) of the Energy Efficiency Directive 2012/27/EU." *Report from the European Commission to the European Parliament and the Council,* July 20. Retrieved from Eur-Lex. https://eur-lex.europa.eu/legal-content/EN/TXT/?qid=1595408944398&uri=CELEX:52020DC0326.

European Commission. n.d. "Ecodesign for Sustainable Products Regulation." Accessed April 30, 2024. https://commission.europa.eu/energy-climate-change-environment/standards-tools-and-labels/products-labelling-rules-and-requirements/sustainable-products/ecodesign-sustainable-products-regulation_en.

European Commission. 2021. "Environmental Footprint Methods." December 16. https://environment.ec.europa.eu/news/environmental-footprint-methods-2021-12-16_en.

European Environment Agency. n.d. "Internalisation of Externalities." Accessed March 3, 2024. www.eea.europa.eu/help/glossary/eea-glossary/internalisation-of-externalities.

Falk, J. and M. Mendiluce. n.d. "The SME Climate Hub Expands its Global Footprint." *SME Climate Hub June Newsletter.* Accessed July 20, 2021. https://us1.campaign-archive.com/?u=644b7786dc2ece10460f9f1b2&id=9274b42335.

FEMA. n.d. "Stay In Business After a Disaster by Planning Ahead."

Federal Office for the Environment FOEN. n.d. "Swiss Emissions Trading Registry." Accessed April 15, 2024. www.emissionsregistry.admin.ch/crweb/public/auction/dates.action?token=IY2RSQKZYM1BHDFCR87Q8N4SQBYP7W2F.

Flood C. 2021. "ETFs Present 'Recipe for Climate Chaos' Study Claims," *Financial Times,* April 21. www-ft-com.ezp-prod1.hul.harvard.edu/content/8ee2ac80-9025-4dbb-bd1c-b33a86e87549.

Folk E. 2019. "10 Ways Renewable Energy Can Save Businesses Money." *Renewable Energy Magazine,* February 8. www.renewableenergymagazine.com/emily-folk/10-ways-renewable-energy-can-save-businesses-20190208.

GE. 2014. "GE Works: 2013 Annual Report." *Letter to Shareowners.* www.ge.com/jp/sites/www.ge .com.jp/files/GE_AR13.pdf.

The Global Goals. n.d. "The 17 Goals. " Accessed March 25, 2024. www.globalgoals.org/goals/.

Global Reporting Initiative (GRI). n.d. "GRI 3: Material Topics 2021." Accessed April 8, 2024. https://globalreporting.org/pdf.ashx?id=12453&page=19.

Google.org. n.d. "Google.org Impact Challenge on Climate 2020. " Accessed July 20, 2021. https://impactchallenge.withgoogle.com/climate2020/charities.

Graham J. 2021. "Net-zero emissions targets adopted by one-fifth of world's largest companies. *Reuters,* March 23, 2021. www.reuters.com/article/us-global-climate-carbon-business-trfn/net-zero-emissions-targets-adopted-by-one-fifth-of-worlds-largest-companies-idUSKBN2BF2ZX.

Greenhouse Gas Protocol. n.d. "Calculation Tools and Guidance. " Accessed April 8, 2024. https://ghgprotocol.org/calculation-tools.

Greenhouse Gas Protocol. n.d. "Scope 3 Calculation Guidance. " Accessed January 30, 2024. https://ghgprotocol.org/scope-3-calculation-guidance-2.

Greenpeace. n.d. "Exxon's Climate Denial History: A Timeline."

Griffin, P., Dr. 2017. "The Carbon Majors Database. " *CDP Worldwide.* https://bit.ly/3wPli6Y2.

Gutoskey E. 2024. "How to Use Your Own Cup for Starbucks Drive-Thru and Mobile Orders. " in Mental Floss. January 9. www.mentalfloss.com/posts/how-to-use-recycled-cups-starbucks-drive-thru-mobile-orders.

Harris, S. and D. Wei. 2018. "Why Climate Resilience Go Hand in Hand." *Business for Social Responsibility (blog).* September 10. www.bsr.org/en/our-insights/blog-view/climate-change-supply-chains-go-hand-in-hand.

Henisz W. , T. Koller., and R. Nuttall. 2019. "Five Ways That ESG Creates Value." *McKinsey Quarterly ,* November. www.mckinsey.com/business-functions/strategy-and-corporate-finance/our-insights/five-ways-that-esg-creates-value?cid=soc-web. Copyright (c) 2021 McKinsey & Company.

High-Level Expert Group on the Net Zero Emissions Commitments of Non-State Entities. 2022. "Integrity Matters: Net Zero Commitments by Businesses, Financial Institutions, Cities and Regions," 17. www.un.org/sites/un2.un.org/files/high-levelexpertgroupupdate7.pdf.

Hill, T. 2020. "Vodafone Embeds Environmental Criteria into Its Supplier Selection Process. " BusinessGreen, September 23, 2020, www.businessgreen.com/news/4020580/vodafone-embeds-environmental-criteria-supplier-selection-process.

Hirst, D. and M. Keep. 2018. "Carbon Price Floor (CPF) and the Price Support Mechanism." January 8. https://commonslibrary.parliament.uk/research-briefings/sn05927/.

H&M Group. n.d. "Circularity." Accessed April 3, 2024. https://hmgroup.com/sustainability/circularity-and-climate/circularity/.

Holmes, T. 2020. "38% of Americans Are Currently Boycotting a Company, and Many Cite Political and Coronavirus Pandemic-Related Reasons." *LendingTree,* July 20, 2020. www.lendingtree.com/credit-cards/study/boycotting-companies-political-pandemic-reasons/.

Hotten, R. 2015. "Volkswagen: The Scandal Explained." BBC News, 10 December. www.bbc.com/news/business-34324772.

Huntington, S. 2020. "Is Climate Change Having an Impact on Manufacturing?" *Alt Energy Mag,* January 22. www.altenergymag.com/article/2020/01/is-climate-change-having-an-impact-on-manufacturing/32543.

Hydrogen Council. n.d. "Why Hydrogen?" Accessed March 6, 2024. https://hydrogencouncil.com/en/why-hydrogen/.

IKEA. n.d. "Designing for a Circular Future." Accessed April 3, 2024. www.ikea. com/global/en/our-business/people-planet/designing-for-a-circular-future/.

Inter-American Development Bank (IDB). 2019. "The Most Unexpected Effect of Climate Change," July 22. www.iadb.org/en/story/most-unexpected-effect-climate-change.

Intergovernmental Panel on Climate Change (IPCC). n.d. "Climate Change 2022. Mitigation of Climate Change. Summary for Policy Makers." Accessed April 8, 2024. www.ipcc.ch/report/ar6/wg3/downloads/report/IPCC_AR6_WGIII_SPM.pdf.

Intergovernmental Panel on Climate Change. n.d. "Global Warming of 1.5°C." Accessed July 20, 2021. www.ipcc.ch/sr15/.

International Energy Agency (IEA). n.d. "Direct Air Capture." Accessed April 30, 2024 www.iea.org/energy-system/carbon-capture-utilisation-and-storage/direct-air-capture.

International Energy Agency. n.d. "Combining Bioenergy With CCS. " Accessed February 23, 2024.www.iea.org/reports/combining-bioenergy-with-ccs.

International Renewable Energy Agency (IRENA). 2020. "Renewable Power Generation Costs in 2019." www.irena.org/publications/2020/Jun/Renewable-Power-Costs-in-2019.

International Standards Organization. "ISO 14044:2006 Environmental Management. Life Cycle Assessment."

International Standards Organization (ISO). n.d. "IWA 42:2022(en) Net Zero Guidelines." Accessed April 8, 2024. www.iso.org/obp/ui/en/#iso:std:iso:iwa:42:ed-1:v1:en.

Johnstone, M.L. and L.P. Tan. August 15, 2015. "Exploring the Gap Between Consumers' Green Rhetoric and Purchasing Behaviour." *Journal of Business Ethics* 132: 311–328.

Kaufman, L. 2024. "Florida's Home Insurance Industry May Be Worse Than Anyone Realizes." April 24. https://finance.yahoo.com/news/florida-home-insurance-industry-may-110021317.html.

Konrad, J. 2019. "Maersk Triple-E—A Detailed Look at The World's Biggest Ship." May 28. https://gcaptain.com/maersk-triple-e-detailed/.

Kruger, J. 2017. "Hedging an Uncertain Future: Internal Carbon Prices in the Electric Power Sector." *Resources for the Future,* April 2017. https://media.rff.org/archive/files/document/file/RFF-Rpt-Kruger-Internal%20Carbon%20Pricing.pdf.

Kuykendall, T. 2020. "Coal Producer Peabody Faces Big Challenges as Potential 2nd Bankruptcy Looms." *S&P Global Market Intelligence*, November 27. www.spglobal.com/marketintelligence/en/news-insights/latest-news-headlines/coal-producer-peabody-faces-big-challenges-as-potential-2nd-bankruptcy-looms-61479849.

Laville. n.d. "Top Oil Firms Spending Millions Lobbying to Block Climate Change Policies."

The LEGO Group. 2024. "RePlay." Accessed April 30, 2024. www.lego.com/ en-us/sustainability/environment/replay?locale=en-us.

Lippincott. n.d. "How to Grow When Markets Don't: Webinar Series Rewind." Accessed July 20, 2021. https://lippincott.com/insight/webinar-rewind/.

Maguire,G. 2024. "US Thermal Coal Exports Hit 5-year Highs and Top $5 Billion in 2023." *Reuters*, February 1. www.reuters.com/markets/commodities/us-thermal-coal-exports-hit-5-year-highs-top-5-billion-2023-2024-02-01/.

Market Research Future. 2020. "Global Green Buildings Market Overview," February.    www.marketresearchfuture.com/reports/green-building-market-4982.

Manfredi, V.M. n.d. *Alexander: Child of a Dream.*

Matsakis, L. 2019. "Thousands of Tech Workers Join Global Climate Change Strike." *Wired,* September 28. www.wired.com/story/tech-workers-global-climate-change-strike/.

Meijer, B. 2024. "Shell says landmark emissions ruling won't help climate goals. " *Reuters*. April 2, 2024. www.reuters.com/business/environment/dutch-court-hears-shells-appeal-against-landmark-climate-ruling-2024-04-02/.

Millani. 2019. "The Role of CDP Disclosure to Improve Access to Capital. " October 2019.   www.millani.ca/_files/ugd/66e92b_90478f727e56463ebd4 0ec1339989eec.pdf.

Milliken, D. M. John, and F. Kerry. 2021. "G7 Backs Making Climate Risk Disclosure Mandatory," *Reuters,* June 5, 2021. www.reuters. com/business/environment/g7-backs-making-climate-risk-disclosure-mandatory-2021-06-05/.

McMillin, D. 2024. CNET Money. "Want a More Energy-Efficient Home? A Green Mortgage Can Help You Pay for It. " March 18, 2024. www.cnet.com/ personal-finance/mortgages/advice/what-is-a-green-mortgage/.

Mollman, S. 2023. "Blockbuster 'Laughed us out of the Room.' Recalls Netflix Cofounder on Trying to Sell Company Now Worth Over $150 Billion for $50 Million." *YahooFinance*, April 16. https://finance. yahoo.com/news/blockbuster-laughed-us-room-recalls-174322621. html?guccounter=1&guce_referrer=aHR0cHM6Ly9kdWNrZHVja2dvLm NvbS8&guce_referrer_sig=AQAAAC9LdfW6RYy2CreCdQDeN8B408 Cgc1GMmqJDHfPD-ESSEqYukbZwYYCX9lxzMknKgJ8qsoFMq N3EcKOyjBoWF14qarBcFXnax__fCHGcrVyYr8bVv_0Bqf7ELCwbOs Y2vUkUPq9RMsdCa0ncCXnVmAHhqEYxvjJcfHHtHZVkNkI6.

Moody's. 2021. "Moody's 2019 Corporate Social Responsibility Report." Accessed July 20. www.moodys.com/sites/products/ProductAttachments/ CSR/Moodys_2020_TCFD_Report.pdf.

National Retail Federation. n.d. "Meet the 2020 Consumers Driving Change." Accessed January 20, 2024. https://nrf.com/research/meet-2020-consumers-driving-change.

Nellis, S. 2017. "Salesforce Acts on Climate, Requiring Suppliers to Set Carbon Goals," *Reuters*, April 29. www.reuters.com/business/sustainable-business/salesforce-acts-climate-requiring-suppliers-set-carbon-goals-2021-04-29/.

Nespresso. 2024. "Responsibility Meets Recyclability." Accessed April 30, 2024. www.nespresso.com/us/en/how-to-recycle-coffee-capsules.

Nurse, D. 2019. "2019 Top 10 Renewable Utilities—Solar and Wind Project Pipeline Analysis." *Energy Acuity*, July 29. www.energyacuity.com/blog/2019-top-10-renewable-utilities-solar-wind/.

NYC Accelerator. n.d. "LOCAL LAW 97. " Accessed April 8, 2024. https://accelerator.nyc/ll97.

Park and Noh. n.d. "Climate Change Risk and Cost of Capital."

Parker, M. 2018. "Letter to Shareholders." *NIKE. Inc*, July 24. https://s1.q4cdn.com/806093406/files/ doc_financials/2018/ar/docs/nike-shareholders-letter-2018.pdf.

Patagonia. 2024. "Introducing the New Footprint Chronicles on Patagonia.com. " Accessed March 23. www.patagonia.com/stories/introducing-the-new-footprint-chronicles-on-patagoniacom/story-18443.html.

Patagonia WornWear. n.d. Accessed April 30, 2024. https://wornwear.patagonia.com/.

Perkins R. and K. Goliya . 2021. "Oil Majors' Credit Ratings Under Threat From Growing Climate Risks: S&P Global. " January 26. www.spglobal.com/commodityinsights/en/market-insights/latest-news/oil/012621-oil-majors-credit-ratings-under-threat-from-growing-climate-risks-sampp-global.

Pigou C. 1920. "The Economics of Welfare."Poisson, M. n.d. "The ESG Data Revolution." *MCMF Publishing*, 84.

Novelli, P. 2022. "The Purpose Priorities Report: How to Respond in the New Era of Accountability. " Porternovelli, October. www.porternovelli.com/wp-content/uploads/2022/10/PPI-Report_04102022.pdf.

Pryor, J. and V Ramana Putti . "Carbon Pricing: Almost 25% of Emissions now Covered Globally, but Coverage and Prices Must Rise Further. " *Energy Post*, October 16. https://energypost.eu/carbon-pricing-almost-25-of-emissions-now-covered-globally-but-coverage-and-prices-must-rise-further/.

Randall, C. 2024. "What Is behind the Success of Electric Buses in the UK." *Electrive*, February 23. www.electrive.com/2024/02/23/whats-behind-the-success-of-electric-buses-in-the-uk/.

Regional Greenhouse Gas Initiative (RGGI, Inc.). n.d. "RGGI 2022 Program Highlights." Accessed December 2. www.rggi.org/.

Reuters. 2024. "UK Supermarket Sainsbury's Launches EV Charging Business." January 11. www.reuters.com/world/uk/uk-supermarket-sainsburys-launches-ev-charging-business-2024-01-12/.

Ridepanda. n.d. Accessed April 30, 2024. www.ridepanda.com/.

Riley. n.d. "100 Companies Responsible For 71% of Global Emissions."

Roach. n.d. "Top 50 Asset Managers created Internal ESG Ratings."

The Rockefeller Foundation. n.d. "100 Resilient Cities." Accessed April 30, 2024. www.rockefellerfoundation.org/100-resilient-cities/.

Ryor, J. 2014. "Shifting to Renewable Energy Can Save U.S. Consumers Money." *World Resources Institute.* June 18. www.wri.org/insights/shifting-renewable-energy-can-save-us-consumers-money.

Sabin Center for Climate Change Law. n.d. "Milieudefensie et al. v. Royal Dutch Shell plc.," Accessed on May 15, 2024. https://climatecasechart.com/non-us-case/milieudefensie-et-al-v-royal-dutch-shell-plc/#:~:text=Four%20days%20of%20hearings%20were,emissions%20and%20end%2Duse%20emissions.

Schreiber, M. 2021. "Addressing Climate Change Concerns in Practice. " *American Psychological Association.* March 1. www.apa.org/monitor/2021/03/ce-climate-change.

Science Based Targets. n.d. "Companies Taking Action." Accessed April 8, 2024. https://sciencebasedtargets.org/companies-taking-action#anchor-link-test.

Science Based Targets. n.d. "Set a Target. " Accessed April 8, 2024. https://sciencebasedtargets.org/step-by-step-process#develop-a-target.

Scriven, G. 2020. "The Great Disrupter. " *The Economist.* September 17. www.economist.com/special-report/2020/09/17/the-great-disrupter.

Sharma, R.K., S. Kumar, K. Vatta, J. Dhillon, and K.N. Reddy. September 2022. "Impact of Recent Climate Change on Cotton and Soybean Yields in the Southeastern United States. " *Journal of Agriculture and Food Research* 9. www.sciencedirect.com/science/article/pii/S2666154322000813#:~:text=A%201%20%C2%B0C%20rise,decreasing%20soybean%20yield%20by%2031.6%25.

Shelton Group. n.d. "Ecopulse™ 2017 Special Report United We Understand. " Accessed April 30, 2024. https://storage.googleapis.com/shelton-group/Pulse%20Reports/EcoPulse%202017%20Special%20Report.pdf.

Silverstein, K. 2022. "Google Has Invested $3.5 Billion in Renewable Energy Projects Worldwide." May 26. www.environmentenergyleader.com/2022/05/google-has-invested-3-5-billion-in-renewable-energy-projects-worldwide/#:~:text=Indeed%2C%20power%20purchase%20agreements%2C%20or,That's%20a%20%243.5%20billion%20investment.

Simon, J.L. 1996. "The Ultimate Resource 2." *Princeton University Press.*

Shellenberger, M. 2020. *Apocalypse Never: Why Environmental Alarmism Hurts Us All.* Harper.  Smith, V. 2020. "2020 TCFD Report: Our Climate

Risk Disclosure." *Citi (blog)*.    December    17.    https://blog.citigroup.
com/2020/12/2020-tcfd-report-our-climate-risk-disclosure/.

Stevenson, D. 2023. "Infrastructure investment trusts: a long-term bet. " July 12.
www.ft.com/content/6803b991-fdfa-4003-852b-3b2e77df9be2.

Chris Stokel-Walker, C. 2019. "Only Extreme Eco-Taxes on Flights Will Change
Our Flying Habits. " in *Wired*, July 12. www.wired.com/story/plane-tax-eco-
france-sweden/.

Sustainable Development Goals. 2024. "SDG Indicators." Accessed March 25,
2024. https://unstats.un.org/sdgs/indicators/indicators-list/.

The Strategic Sourceror. 2019."Walmart Rewarding Sustainable Suppliers
with Better Financing From HSBC. " April 29. www.strategicsourceror.
com/2019/04/walmart-rewarding-sustainable-suppliers.html.

Swiss Re Group. 2021. "World Economy Set to Lose Up to 18% GDP From
Climate Change if no Action Taken, Reveals Swiss Re Institute's Stress-Test
Analysis. " April 22. www.swissre.com/media/news-releases/nr-20210422-
economics-of-climate-change-risks.html.

Tamny, J. 2021. "A Free-Market Defense of Coca-Cola, Delta, and
'Woke' Capitalism. " *Forbes*.    April    25.    www.forbes.com/sites/
johntamny/2021/04/25/a-free-market-defense-of-coca-cola-delta-and-woke-
capitalism/?sh=42ddf0255198.

Tarbaton, R. 2019. "If Companies Want to Meet Climate Targets, They Must Take
Employees on the Journey." *Reuters Events*. February 28. www.reutersevents.
com/sustainability/if-companies-want-meet-climate-targets-they-must-take-
employees-journey.

Task Force on Climate-Related Financial Disclosures (TCFD). n.d. "TCFD
Recommendations. " Accessed April 30, 2024. www.fsb-tcfd.org/
recommendations/.

Taylor, C. A. Foyn and R. Skinner. 2023 . "Green Quadrant: Climate Change
Consultinting. " June 27. www.verdantix.com/report/green-quadrant-
climate-change-consulting-2023.

Taylor, C. and R. Skinner. 2023. "Global Corporate Survey 2023: Net Zero
Budgets, Priorities and Tech Preferences." *Verdantix*. April 4. www.verdantix.
com/report/global-corporate-survey-2023-net-zero-budgets-priorities-and-
tech-preferences.

Tesla. n.d. "Powerwall." Accessed April 30, 2024. www.tesla.com/powerwall.

Threlfall, R. A. King, W. Bartels, J. Shulman, and M. Hayes. 2020. "Towards
Net Zero." *KPMG*. November. https://assets.kpmg/content/dam/kpmg/xx/
pdf/2020/11/towards-net-zero.pdf.

Toffel, M. and J, Macomber. 2024. "Building Climate—Resilient Cities and
Infrastructure. " *Harvard Business School, Climate Rising Podcast*. March 27.
www.hbs.edu/environment/podcast/Pages/default.aspx.

Toyota. n.d. "Vehicle Life Cycle Assessments." Accessed March 4, 2024. www.toyota-europe.com/sustainability/carbon-neutrality/vehicle-life-cycle-assessments.

Ubuntoo. n.d. "We Use Collective Intelligence to Solve The Planet's Biggest Challenges." Accessed April 8, 2024. https://ubuntoo.com/.

Unilever. n.d. "Our Climate Transition Action Plan. " Accessed April 30, 2024. www.unilever.com/sustainability/climate/our-climate-transition-action-plan/.

Unilever. n.d. "Unilever Sustainable Agriculture Code." Accessed April 30, 2024. www.unilever.com/files/a3f52ce3-22f7-4048-9c5b-55fa3a7895c4/ul-sac-v1-march-2010-spread.pdf.

Union of Concerned Scientists. "A Climate of Corporate Control."

United Nations Environmental Program (UNEP). n.d. "Resource Efficiency." Accessed April 29, 2024. www.unep.org/explore-topics/resource-efficiency.

United Nations Framework Convention on Climate Change. 2020. "Commitments to Net Zero Double in Less Than a Year." September 21. https://unfccc.int/news/commitments-to-net-zero-double-in-less-than-a-year.

U.S. Commodity Futures Trading Commission. 2020. "Managing Climate Risk in the U.S. Financial System." Report of the Climate-Related Market Risk Subcommittee. September 2020. https://bit.ly/3zjCfYP.

US Department of Energy. n.d. "Better Buildings. " Accessed April 8, 2024. https://betterbuildingssolutioncenter.energy.gov/financing-navigator/option/power-purchase-agreement?ref=ctvc.co.

U.S. Department of Energy. n.d. "Solid-State Lighting Program. Accessed February 5, 2024. www.energy.gov/eere/ssl/solid-state-lighting.

U.S. Energy Information Administration. n.d. "Biomass Explained. " Accessed March 4, 2024. www.eia.gov/energyexplained/biomass/.

U.S. Environmental Protection Agency (EPA). n.d. "Climate Change Indicators: Atmospheric Concentrations of Greenhouse Gases. " Accessed April 8, 2024. www.epa.gov/climate-indicators/climate-change-indicators-atmospheric-concentrations-greenhouse-gases#:~:text=Carbon%20dioxide%20concentrations%20have%20increased,is%20due%20to%20human%20activities.

United States Environmental Protection Agency. 2021. "Learn About the Greenhouse Gas Reporting Program (GHGRP)" EPA.gov. March 2. www.epa.gov/ghgreporting/learn-about-greenhouse-gas-reporting-program-ghgrp.

U.S. Environmental Protection Agency (EPA). n.d. "Smart Steps to Sustainability 2.0. " Accessed April 8, 2024. www.epa.gov/sites/default/files/documents/smart_steps_greening_guide.pdf.

U.S. Securities and Exchange Commission. 2021. "SEC Announces Enforcement Task Force Focused on Climate and ESG Issues." March 4. www.sec.gov/news/press-release/2021-42.

We Mean Business Coalition. September 21, 2014. "The Climate Has Changed." www.wemeanbusinesscoalition.org/blog/the-climate-has-changed/.

Whelan T. and Fink C. 2016. "The Comprehensive Business Case for Sustainability." *Harvard Business Review,* October 21. https://hbr.org/2016/10/the-comprehensive-business-case-for-sustainability.

The White House Historical Association. "When was Electricity First Installed at The White House?" Accessed May 5, 2025. whitehousehistorical.org

William A. Taylor 1988. *What Every Engineer should know about Artificial Intelligence.* Cambridge, London: The MIT Press, p 259.

Zhang, Peng, Olivier Deschenes, Kyle Meng, and Junjie Zhang. March 2018. "Temperature Effects on Productivity and Factor Reallocation: Evidence From a Half Million Chinese Manufacturing Plants," *Journal of Environmental Economics and Management* 88: 1–17. https://doi.org/10.1016/j.jeem.2017.11.001.

# About the Author

**Valentina Fomenko** is a dynamic force in corporate and sustainability strategy, blending entrepreneurial vision with a desire for practical impact. She has consulted for public and private sector organizations across more than 20 industries—including the World Bank and the UN Development Program—and supports leaders in integrating sustainability into the very core of business operations. Valentina holds an M.S. in Environmental Sciences and Policy from Central European University, a Ph.D. in Environmental Science from Oregon State University, and an MBA from Duke University's Fuqua School of Business. Outside of work, she is a passionate gardener—an expression of her deep commitment to regeneration and living in harmony with natural systems.

# Index

Aeon Group, 76
Air France, 95
Airlock Insulation, 80
Artificial intelligence (AI), 103, 107

BASF, 41
Bezos, J., 103
Big Oil, 90
BloombergNEF, 78–79

Canada's Oil Sands Innovation
    Alliance (COSIA), 125
Carbon Border Adjustment
    Mechanism (CBAM), 6
Carbon capture and utilization
    (CCU), 32–33
Carbon credits, 23, 102, 105, 106
Carbon dioxide ($CO_2$) emissions, 5,
    12, 17, 18, 24, 25, 33, 36, 48,
    76, 79, 104
Carbon disclosure management, 23
Carbon footprint, 1, 6, 9, 10, 17–23,
    26–28, 30–34, 40, 42, 43,
    46–52, 61, 68, 69, 76–78,
    80, 81, 95–97, 102, 104, 105,
    115, 116, 119
Carbon goals, 35–37
Carbon offset, 24, 33–37, 69–70,
    85–86, 105
Carbon pricing, 23–26, 70, 85, 95
Carbon sequestration, 33, 87
Chevron, 32
Circular economy, 30–31, 49, 51, 90
Citizens' Climate Lobby et al. v.
    Chevron et al. (2020), 61
Climate adaptation, 73, 74, 82,
    86–87, 99, 101, 122
Climate anxiety, 83, 142
Climate Disclosure Project (CDP), 1,
    6, 7, 9–13, 22, 39, 41, 46, 48,
    75, 88
Climate Disclosure Standards Board
    (CDSB), 7

Climate opportunity, 73–75
    changing markets, 83–86
    cutting operating costs, 88–91
    decarbonization, 79–80
    lower-emission energy sources,
        78–79
    products and services, 80–83
    resilience, 86–87
    resource efficiency, 75–78
Climate ratings, 8–9
Climate Registry, 105
Climate risks, 10, 57–58
    assessment, 63–65
    4°C scenario, 67–68
    liability risks, 61–62
    management, 69–72
    physical risks, 58–59
    reputational risks, 63
    stock prices decline, 65–67
    transition risks, 59–61
    "well below 2°C" or 1.5°C scenario,
        68
Climate strategy, 1, 3, 7–11, 15, 71,
    96–99, 101, 103, 104, 125,
    126, 137, 139
Climate Transition Action Plan, 76
Climate tzar, 100
Coca-Cola, "World Without Waste,"
    77
Communities, 126–128
Communities Around the World v. BP
    (2023), 61
Competitors and industry
    organizations, 125–126
CoolClimate Network, 19
Corporate strategy failure, 137–138
Corporate Sustainability Reporting
    Directive (CSRD), 6
COVID-19 pandemic, 13, 74, 129,
    142
Cruz Foam, 77
Customer engagement, 50–53,
    116–119

Danone, 25, 48
Data and analytics, 102–103
Decarbonization, 12, 79–80
    plan, 53, 96–98, 105, 137, 139
Decarbonization levers, 26
    carbon offsetting, 33–34
    CCU technologies, 32–33
    energy efficiency, 27
    fuel switching, 29–30
    process optimization, 28
    renewable energy, 28–29
    transportation decarbonization,
        31–32
    waste reduction and circular
        economy, 30–31
Dell, 31
Dow Chemical Company, 76
Duke Energy, 29

Earth Charter, 134–135
Ecochain, 44
Electric vehicles (EVs) and markets,
    81, 83–85, 90
Emissions trading system (EU ETS),
    24
Employee engagement, 114–116
Energy efficiency, 27, 33–34, 51, 67,
    76–78, 83, 85, 95, 97–98,
    125
Environmental nonprofits, 122–124
Environmental, Social, and
        Governance (ESG) function,
        15, 16, 86–87, 107, 113,
        135
Esser, V., 13
European Green Deal, 6
European Union (EU), 6, 15, 24, 26,
    41, 95
Externalities (internalization of),
    94–95
External stakeholders, 116–128
    See also Stakeholders

Financial control, 20
Financial risks, 70
4°C scenario, 67–68
Fuel switching, 29–30

General electric, 76
Global ESG Benchmark for Real
        Assets (GRESB), 8
Global warming, 5, 36, 84
    global warming potential (GWP), 17
GreenBiz, 4
Green Building Institute, 78
Greenhouse gas (GHG) emissions,
    2, 5–7, 9, 12–15, 17, 19–21,
    25, 46, 48, 94–98, 104, 122,
    124–125
Greenhouse Gas Protocol, 18–19
Greenhouse Gas Reporting Program
        (GHGRP), 5
Green purchasing gap, 118
Green rate programs, 29
Gross domestic product (GDP) loss, 3

Hauff, J., 127
H&M, 31

IKEA, 30–31, 86
Intergovernmental Panel on Climate
        Change (IPCC), 3, 18, 36, 67
Internal stakeholders, 112–116
    See also Stakeholders
International Energy Agency, xi
Investors and lenders, 120–122
ISO 31,000: Risk Management
        standard, 69

LED lights, 27, 76, 89, 104, 127
Liability risks, 61–62
Life cycle assessment (LCA)
    conducting, 42–46, 104
    value of, 40–42

Maersk, 77
Manfredi, V. M., 13
McKinsey & Company, 75
Mean Business Coalition, 123
Milieudefensie v. Royal Dutch Shell
        (2023), 61

Nestlé, 71
Net-zero emissions, 23, 25, 35–37,
        78, 97, 99, 105

NextEra Energy, 79
Nike, 117

Oil and gas companies, 90
Operational control, 19–20
Operational risks, 70
Organization and staffing, 100–102
O'Sullivan, D., 71

Parametric insurance, 78, 82
Patagonia, 40, 51
Peabody Energy, 90
Physical risks, 58–59
Pigou, A., 94
Poisson, M., 86, 107
Policies and procedures, 99–100
Power purchase agreements (PPAs),
    28–29
Process optimization, 28
Product environmental footprint
    (PEF) method, 41

Real Estate Investment Trusts (REITs)
    and property companies, 87
Regional Greenhouse Gas Initiative
    (RGGI), 24
Regulators, 124–125
Renewable energy, 28–29, 60, 69–71,
    73, 76, 78–79, 81, 84–85,
    87, 91, 93, 95, 106, 112, 125,
    128
Renewable Energy Buyers Alliance,
    125–126
Renewable energy credits (RECs), 29
Reputational risks, 63
Resilience, 86–87
Resource efficiency, 75–78
Return on Investment (ROI), 81
Ridepanda, 31–32, 81

Sarbanes–Oxley Act of 2002, 8, 9
Science-based targets (SBTs), 36–37
Science Based Targets initiative
    (SBTi), 7, 36–37
SCRAP NYC, 52
Securities and Exchange Commission
    (SEC), 6

Seitz, U., 82
Shareholders, 112–113
Simon, J., *The Ultimate Resource*, 13
SME Climate Hub, 123
Sorkin, R., 56
Stakeholders, 110–112
    communities, 126–128
    competitors and industry
        organizations, 125–126
    customers, 116–119
    employees, 114–116
    environmental nonprofits, 122–124
    investors and lenders, 120–122
    management, 113–114
    map, 111
    regulators, 124–125
    shareholders, 112–113
    suppliers, 119–120
Stock prices decline, 65–67
Supplier engagement, 47–50, 119–
    120
Sustainability Accounting Standards
    Board (SASB), 7
Sustainable Development Goals
    (SDGs), 135–136

Task Force on Climate-Related
    Financial Disclosures
    (TCFD), 8, 10, 58, 68, 73–74
Tesla, 80, 81, 85, 90
Toyota, 40
Transition risks, 59–61
Transportation emissions/
    decarbonization, 21, 30–32,
    49, 60, 66, 70, 77, 79, 81,
    97, 104
Trayner, G., 13

Ubuntoo, 141
Uncertainty, 56–57, 66, 67, 130, 138,
    144
United States Department of
    Agriculture (USDA), 130
U.S. Green Building Council, 77–78

Verification process, 104–105
Volkswagen, 31, 62

Walmart, 76
Waste reduction, 30–31, 90
"Well below 2°C" or 1.5°C scenario, 68
Wild West of climate change strategy,
    7–11
Winter, O., 27, 50, 115

World Business Council for
    Sustainable Development
    (WBCSD), 123
World Green Building Council
    (WGBC), 122–123
Worn Wear program, 51

www.ingramcontent.com/pod-product-compliance
Lightning Source LLC
Chambersburg PA
CBHW061309220326
41599CB00026B/4794